WORLD-CLASS CUSTOMER SATISFACTION

Jonathan D. Barsky

WORLD-CLASS CUSTOMER SATISFACTION

Jonathan D. Barsky

Professional Publishing
Burr Ridge, Illinois
New York, New York

This publication is designed to provide accurate and authoritative
information in regard to the subject matter covered. It is sold
with the understanding that neither the author or the publisher is
engaged in rendering legal, accounting, or other professional service.
If legal advice or other expert assistance is required, the services
of a competent professional person should be sought.

*From a Declaration of Principles jointly adopted by a Committee
of the American Bar Association and a Committee of Publishers.*

Editor-in-chief:	Jeffrey A. Krames
Marketing manager:	Kate Wickham
Project editor:	Rita McMullen
Production manager:	Ann Cassady
Designer:	Mercedes Santos
Art manager:	Kim Meriwether
Compositor:	Alexander Graphics, Inc.
Typeface:	11/13 Times Roman
Printer:	The Book Press, Inc.

Library of Congress Cataloging-in-Publication Data

Barsky, Jonathan D.
    World-class customer satisfaction / Jonathan D. Barsky.
        p.   cm.
    Includes index.
    ISBN 0-7863-0128-7
    1. Consumer satisfaction—Case studies.   2. Customer service—Case
studies.   I. Title.
    HF5415.5.B37   1995   94-18563
    658.8'12—dc20

Printed in the United States of America
1 2 3 4 5 6 7 8 9 0 BP 1 0 9 8 7 6 5 4

To my world-class parents: Shirley and Morrey Barsky.

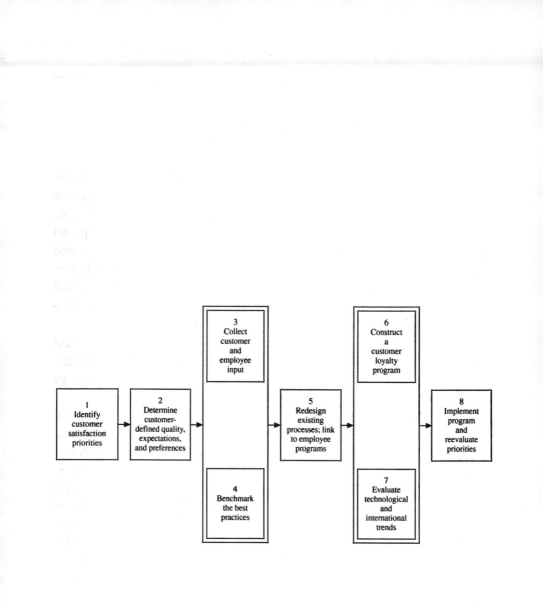

Preface

Customer satisfaction is linked to profitability. Higher levels of customer satisfaction lead to increased profits. Many U.S. companies are using this basic principle to regain the huge market losses that began in the 1970s. The victories are found across our economy—from computer chip and automobile manufacturing to the banking, financial services, and entertainment and recreation industries. The pacesetters in these industries—Intel Corp., Ford, Citicorp, Merrill Lynch, Walt Disney, and Blockbuster—have achieved their comebacks by focusing on and delivering the fundamental elements of customer satisfaction.

We will focus on the techniques that helped these and other world-class companies prosper. The sequence of topics and interactive format of the book will allow you to develop a complete customer satisfaction strategy tailored to your situation.

To remain competitive, organizations no longer rely on traditional ways of satisfying customers. Companies are automating and streamlining complete business functions to improve their ability to please customers. We have studied exceptional companies from the United States, Europe, and Asia to reveal their methods for achieving customer satisfaction. This book is based on research involving approximately 250 organizations known for their innovative and effective approaches to satisfying customers. This included over 50 executive interviews representing 15 countries, numerous surveys, extensive professional work and academic investigations since 1986, and the cooperation and direct contribution from many companies.

These organizations and executives were selected for their ability to consistently deliver the highest levels of customer satisfaction. To be considered for this research program, companies were required to maintain regular use of feedback from all customer segments, input from employees and other operating partners, and regular methods of benefiting from the accomplishments of competitors, not limited by industry boundaries.

World-class customer satisfaction is achieved by drawing from the best management and labor practices in U.S. and overseas companies. Using a wide variety of industry examples, including hotels, restaurants, banks, airlines, and consumer product and manufacturing companies, each chapter defines a problem, highlights current cases, and demonstrates the most crucial steps for building customer satisfaction.

Each chapter centers on several of the core concepts that have proven successful for world-class organizations. These are noted by an icon, as shown here, and represent the underlying principles and practices used by these companies to achieve world-class customer satisfaction. In addition, each chapter contains valuable examples of world-class customer service. These are *Service Wars* and identified by a "server with boxing gloves" icon.

The *World-Class Customer Satisfaction Program* at the end of the book details a practical plan for implementing and delivering a customer satis-faction strategy designed for the needs of your organization.

Satisfying and keeping loyal customers is becoming more complex. In the future, the companies with the most knowledge of their clients will have a competitive advantage. This requires aggressively seeking cus-tomer, employee, and competitor input on a frequent basis. The material presented in this book brings together diverse information that will help you achieve your unique customer satisfaction objectives.

Jonathan D. Barsky

Acknowledgments

No job in my life has ever been accomplished without help, and this one has been no exception. First, I am indebted to Daianne Irigoyen, who with her ingenious ideas and discriminating eye has made a substantial contribution to the core ideas and presentation of this work. Her sound criticism, unfailing encouragement, and detailed responses to countless drafts proved invaluable throughout the development of this book.

I have also benefited from fundamental research assistance provided by Nathalie Bergeron, Stan Bromley, Tina Turner, Richard Labagh, Susan Dittmann, and Vinay Singh. Their tag-team efforts helped propel and sustain this project from its inception in 1987. I owe special thanks and gratitude to my students, who with their fresh ideas and candid appraisals helped shape and refine many of the book's concepts and applications.

To the scores of international business persons, academicians, and public servants, too many to recognize individually, who generously contributed their time and talents—a profound thank-you for your collective wisdom, which is the justification for this book. And to those organizations, associations, and international entities, also too numerous to acknowledge—your inestimable support provided the necessary groundwork to hold this project together.

And most of all, thanks to my colleagues, friends, and family who have provided infinite patience and understanding so necessary to sustain direction and rationality.

J. D. B.

Foreword

Today's economy has forced many businesses to focus on the spreadsheet. The most expedient solution seems to be downsizing and cutting costs to make a business more profitable. All this attention paid to the bottom line has blinded managers to what should be their main focus: the customer. It is the customer who has the power to change the profit/loss figures in an annual report. Only by listening to the customer can one hope to make a solid, lasting, and profitable change in business.

By focusing on the customer, one is really concentrating on serving and satisfying the customer's needs. Customer satisfaction creates customer retention, which in turn means profitability. It sounds like an easy answer, but it involves a commitment—commitment to shift service to the number one priority position. It also means changing the traditional management style: moving decision making from the management level to the frontline employee level.

Customer satisfaction is inextricably linked to profitability—you must keep your customers, and to keep your customers, you must make them happy.

In today's competitive climate, where technology, global travel, and cross-cultural sharing of goods and ideas can homogenize many products, it is service that distinguishes a company, hotel, or manufacturer from another. Service is the component that differentiates a superior product from an average product, an excellent night's stay at a hotel from a merely average night's stay. I believe service is ultimately the key to success or failure for any business.

Today's service means constantly redesigning product and customer service so that customers get what they want. If those needs change, then you have a system in place that tells you quickly how to design new products and services.

Pursuing and then winning the Malcolm Baldrige National Quality Award in 1992 taught us that we cannot remain at one level of customer satisfaction. We must constantly strive to improve ourselves, our service, and our systems because customer satisfaction is not a short-term goal. Customer satisfaction is a never-ending process.

World-Class Customer Satisfaction carries a very important message, one that has value for every organization in every industry. Jonathan Barsky has done an extraordinary job of presenting the tools and techniques of customer satisfaction and showing how any organization can achieve new levels of excellence in a comprehensive approach. With his clear and highly readable explanation of exciting new ideas, Jonathan has made a valuable contribution to contemporary business thinking.

I urge all executives and managers to read this book carefully, reflect on its message, and apply its program in their organization.

Horst S. Schulze
President and Chief Operating Officer
The Ritz-Carlton Hotel Company

Contents

List of Exhibits

Chapter One

The New Customer Imperative
Profit Opportunities of Customer Satisfaction

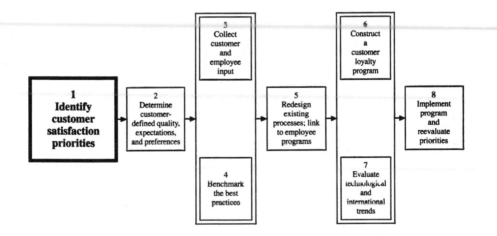

Imagine driving through the south of France in 1904 and your Rolls-Royce breaks down. You call Rolls-Royce in England and the company dispatches a mechanic with a new driveshaft to fix your car. Weeks later, when you call to inquire about the bill, the company claims it has no record of the service taking place. It asserts that "Rolls-Royce motor cars never break down; they sometimes fail to proceed."

This company stood behind its product and went to great effort and expense to do what was necessary to meet its customer's needs. This is an example of how to achieve *world-class customer satisfaction*. Rolls-Royce delivered the products and services that not only provided what was needed but also addressed its customer's personal concerns. The company successfully organized and integrated the traditional functions of marketing, operations, and human resource management to provide a satisfactory service experience.

Customer satisfaction is a feeling. It creates enjoyment and pleasure. It can dazzle, delight, or overwhelm. Lack of satisfaction, however, can cause disappointment and frustration. Both satisfaction and dissatisfaction can affect customers' attitudes toward a product and a service or influence perceptions of an entire organization.

U.S. companies understand the potency of customer satisfaction. It is one of the most widely embraced concepts in business. Eighty-six percent of senior executives from Fortune 500 companies consider customer satisfaction to be extremely important to their company and rank it a higher priority than 10 other goals, including productivity and company reputation.[1] Asian and European managers have similar views.[2]

THE UNRAVELING OF TRADITION

Satisfying customers is not a new idea. At the beginning of this century, Neiman-Marcus, one of the great retailers of all time, changed the doctrine of "let the buyer beware" to "let the buyer decide if he is satisfied." Whereas horse traders often hid defects from buyers, Neiman-Marcus instructed its sales force to "sell satisfaction not just merchandise."

Unfortunately, U.S. business has drifted away from this tradition of service. During the 1970s, American firms, dominated by a production mentality and cost-reduction efforts, did not perceive poor customer satisfaction as a major problem. Leading market research actually supported the notion that the United States was "succeeding reasonably well in providing acceptable levels of satisfaction to the buying public," and that "consumers find enjoyment and satisfaction in their buying experiences . . . considerably more often than they find difficulty and discontent."[3]

As a result, the U.S. population's strong demand for service and products in the last 20 years has been met primarily by technical product innovations rather than by service improvements or other quality considerations.

American industry is still out of touch with the simple things that average Americans really need, use, and buy. Some major industries, such as automobiles and electronics, may be staging comebacks, but poor customer service continues to top the list of customer dissatisfaction across industries.[4] Too many companies still don't get it. One embarrassing example: VCRs are *still* too complicated to program. Would you believe that the fastest growth segment of the home video market is the sale of videocassettes of TV shows, especially those that were presented only a few weeks earlier?

Airlines still overbook, waiters aren't trained to serve people, hospital workers are too busy to provide compassionate care, and resolving a billing error with the phone company takes much too long. These everyday service abuses are so commonplace that they almost go unnoticed. Even the National Restaurant Association admits "slow service" is the major problem at many dining spots in the United States.[5]

WHAT'S THE ANSWER?

"Improve customer satisfaction!" Sound familiar? You've heard it, your neighbor has heard it, your dog has heard it. Over the past several years everybody has heard it, but consumers are still wondering when companies are finally going to deliver real product and service satisfaction.

Corporations have been obsessed with cutting costs, bolstering cash flow, and boosting overall market share. Although they see customer service and satisfaction as critical, they have no idea how to create it and are often intimidated by its apparent complexity. Many manufacturers, service organizations, and public and private institutions have been affected by severe competition and other economic pressures, causing them to lose touch with their customers. For example, people 50 and older represent more than half of the discretionary income in the United States—providing a valuable and growing market for dining and travel. Yet restaurants and hotels continue to light their rooms with 60 watt bulbs—barely enough light to cast a shadow.[6]

Despite the well-publicized failures of some American businesses, there are many others that have achieved superior levels of customer satisfaction. The U.S. companies we selected as world-class examples have adapted and prospered in competitive world markets. These companies have been forced to understand that although tight financial controls, political savvy, and a recognized name may help, they are not sufficient for succeeding in world markets. Making money in today's world economy demands strong leadership, a committed workforce, and, most of all, an intense focus on customers and their needs.

 World-class companies have broadened and accelerated their efforts toward improvement by making significant advances in product and service quality, employee training, and other customer treatment areas.

The concepts and tools presented in this book have proven successful with big and small businesses, government agencies, and universities. For example:

- The Four Season's Hotel in San Francisco used the customer satisfaction scoring method to discover and strengthen weak links in their operation.
- A food distributor found that by surveying deli managers in supermarkets, it could modify or add services to increase business.
- The Seattle Convention and Visitors Bureau used the customer survey system (Chapters 2–3) to assess the satisfaction of their various market segments.
- TARP, a government affiliated agency in Washington DC, is considering this approach to investigate consumer and company practices across a wide variety of U.S. products and services.
- Cornell University and the University of Houston used this approach for evaluating student satisfaction.
- Sheraton used this program in an executive retreat focusing on guest satisfaction.

These techniques may be applied to any business challenge involving a customer. They are effective for large-scale projects as well as for smaller retailers and consumer goods or services producers that want to improve their focus on consumer needs and complaints. The key is to give customer satisfaction a chance to show its value for your organization.

You'll have the opportunity to implement the concepts and tools contained in each chapter using the World-Class Customer Satisfaction Program, detailed in Chapter 8. This systematic application offers a comprehensive approach to improving customer satisfaction in your organization.

BIG PRIZES AWAIT!

In the 1990s, more customers are going to reward the companies that bend over backward to satisfy their needs. Improving customer satisfaction has big payoffs but is extremely hard work. Leon Gorman, president of L.L. Bean, once said that customer service and satisfaction is a "day-in, day-out, ongoing, never-ending, unremitting, persevering, compassionate type of activity."

Some companies have formally correlated their customers' satisfaction with financial performance. IBM in Rochester, New York, found that each additional percentage point in their customer satisfaction scores meant an additional $257 million gain in revenue over a five-year period for this location.

Conversely, using profits alone may not be a true indicator of customer satisfaction. Just because a company shows a profit in the current period does not mean it is winning customers. Too often, cost-containment efforts squeeze out a profit by reducing quality or services and can alienate customers in the process, hurting future profits. Customer satisfaction is an investment with short- and long-term payoffs. This profit potential is demonstrated by Malcolm Baldrige Award winners. This honor, envisioned as a standard of excellence to help U.S. companies compete internationally, is managed by the Department of Commerce and favors those companies that emphasize and obtain high levels of customer satisfaction (Exhibit 1–1).

Customer satisfaction is of interest to business only when it leads to profit. It yields profits in four ways:

1. Increases chances for repeat purchase.
2. Creates positive word-of-mouth promotion.
3. Increases customer expenditure on current purchases.
4. Affects cash flow.

Eight of 10 Fortune 500 companies say the customer service they provide affects customer decisions to pay invoices on time. More than half of the largest U.S. companies say the customer service they receive from a vendor or supplier affects their decision to pay an invoice on time. Moreover, half of the largest U.S. companies (51 percent) have withheld payment to a vendor or supplier because they were dissatisfied with the level of customer service they received.[7]

EXHIBIT 1–1

Malcolm Baldrige Winners Increased Revenue with Customer Satisfaction Emphasis*

Malcolm Baldrige Winners	Annual Sales Growth, 1987–92
Federal Express	237.0%
Motorola	47.0
Wallace	44.4
Xerox	24.0
Texas Instruments	17.0
Granite Rock	15.0
IBM	14.5

*Data came from company reports. The category for customer satisfaction is weighted 30 percent in the Malcolm Baldrige grading criteria, twice as much as any of the other six sections (see Exhibit 1–3).

Satisfying customers is the single best strategy a business can follow to make money. This is because the basic indicators of profitability and customer satisfaction are the same: gaining customer loyalty and market share through word-of-mouth promotion, improved reputation, selling more to current markets, and increasing margins.[8] But just as profit indicators can be misleading, methods supposed to gauge and improve customer satisfaction can also be very deceptive.

 World-class companies understand what satisfies their clientele the most and utilize this information in customer programs and employee training to promote customer loyalty.

For many U.S. firms during the 1970s and 1980s, large-scale cost-reduction efforts and a production mentality severely restricted their ability to satisfy existing customers. These companies met increasing demands with high-tech gadgets and low-cost service extras rather than with significant improvements in product quality and overall customer satisfaction. Cosmetic changes can't compete with efficient market forces and increasingly sophisticated products and services. The hard-learned lesson for these companies was that satisfying customers is what leads to profits and that technical product innovation, small refinements, or expanded marketing budgets alone can't sustain customers.

Service is only part of what it takes to satisfy customers. Good service does not guarantee satisfaction.

SERVICE IS NOT SATISFACTION

A fundamental barrier to servicing customer needs is the misunderstanding of the term *customer satisfaction*. Quality, customer service, and customer satisfaction are very different concepts. For example, quality is a prime cut of beef; customer service is cooking the steak at the table; and customer satisfaction is a customer enjoying the experience (the quality and service) enough to return to the restaurant.

Too often companies engage in "amenity wars"—adding accessories or frills that really don't alter the core value of the product or service. These efforts are as futile as offering trading stamps to attract and keep customers.

Airlines offer similar service embellishments. Foreign carriers have tried to woo the lucrative Japanese business travelers by promising big improvements in meals and other services. These included serving hot sake, rice, and vinegar octopus in gray, lacquered boxes; airing Japanese TV news; offering Japanese language word processors; and even assigning staff to foreign airports to assist the Japanese upon arrival. But these promotions didn't sustain the demanding Japanese business person because they were not accompanied by what Japanese travelers look for in an airline: efficiency and value. Customers soon returned to the more dependable Japan Airlines (JAL).

Service Wars
Nordstrom employees in their Alaska store will warm up customers' cars as they're finishing their shopping.

Good service does not ensure customer satisfaction. Improved service may bolster sales in the short term. But competitors may introduce similar or other service enhancements that may eliminate a firm's competitive advantage. This cat-and-mouse approach to service is the basis for most firms' service strategy. The better approach is to determine whether improved service increases overall satisfaction and repeat business. How long should the services be continued? Are they cost-effective to continue? Finding the answers to these questions (see Chapter 2) is difficult; but remember, service is only part of what it takes to satisfy customers.

Although some sellers continue to come up with innovative services, enduring success will come to those that can maintain the essential product while delivering added services customers value.

Service Wars
Business travelers are finally getting practical services from the hotel industry. Express check-in and checkout, two phone lines, data ports, and functional desks are becoming standard. Hyatt offers guests an in-room fax machine, a free telephone calling card, continental breakfast, and two telephones for $15 above the regular rate.

Some companies have been able to sustain the quality of their core products and services while providing new, value-added offerings to their customers. These world-class companies are known for their customer focus and often outperform others in their industry. Examples include Federal Express, Motorola, Wallace, Xerox, Texas Instruments, Granite Rock, IBM, Southwest Airlines, Saturn, Wal-Mart, Nordstrom Stores, Four Season's Hotels, L.L. Bean, Neiman Marcus, and Hewlett-Packard. Despite worldwide economic weakness, customer-driven firms have shown big revenue increases with strong profits (see Exhibit 1–1).

Companies known for customer satisfaction outperform others in their industry.

START NOW

The first step is to focus on your company (or department, big or small), looking to see how any of this can apply to your situation. The objective is to take advantage of an opportunity or confront a problem that is critical to

EXHIBIT 1–2
Internal Barriers To Customer Satisfaction*

Barrier	Description	Example	Solution
Product	Product or service delivered does not meet or exceed customer expectations.	Hardware supplies at Price Club stores sold for retail prices.	Chapter 2
Personnel	Personality and individual employee's characteristics restrict or prevent customer satisfaction.	Office workers at Epic records have an arrogant, "I don't have time for you" attitude.	Chapter 5
Bureaucratic	Policies, procedures, and rules impede customer satisfaction.	Getting a refund from any Emporium Department store may be routed through Phoenix, Arizona, and numerous other internal control steps.	Chapter 5
Technology	Production-based innovations or service technologies restrict customer objectives.	Calling companies often requires listening to more than 10 rings and being asked to "hold" by a machine.	Chapter 7
Managerial	Lack of desire or effort to support customer orientation.	Most airlines do not provide comment cards, and when they do, it's a hassle to request them.	Chapter 6
Cost-related	Insufficient expenditures dedicated to customer objectives.	El Torito restaurants charge for extra sour cream on fajitas.	Chapter 3

*See Exhibit 5–3 for general solutions to each of these barriers.

your organization. To narrow the scope of issues that can affect customer satisfaction, look at the general barriers that can restrict efforts to please customers (Exhibit 1–2). Which barriers could be holding your company back?

Internal barriers can seriously reduce a company's ability to provide necessary levels of customer satisfaction. These can include troublesome hurdles such as low quality products and services designed without the customer in mind, or employees who have never received one minute of coaching or training. Other damaging barriers can be management's over-zealous concern with established operating procedures, poorly chosen technical improvements, or the always popular "We can't afford it!" excuse. However, these problems can be overcome.

A firm can reduce barriers within the organization by using the "internal customer" concept. Some employees not directly servicing the public may say, "We don't have any customers." But they do; all employees do. The Japanese introduced the notion that there are both external and internal customers. The internal customer is the employee who receives and uses the output from another person or area. Treating this relationship with the same respect and attention given the external customer relationship is the focus of the internal customer concept. If you're in manufacturing, for example, and you have to hand your finished product to distribution, then distribution is your internal customer. Distribution then has to turn to customer service to set up installation of the product; hence, customer service is distribution's internal customer. It's very important that all employees understand and actually practice this next-in-line concept.

 An internal customer is the employee who receives and uses output from another person or area. The internal customer concept means treating internal customers with a similar level of respect and attention that external customers receive.

We'll confront the internal barriers to customer satisfaction separately throughout the book. First, we'll present two customer-based techniques, examining the customer service cycle and obtaining customer feedback, through which you can identify barriers restricting your ability to satisfy customers. Next, we'll discuss how to identify which barriers are the most crucial. Finally, we'll suggest how to correct the weaknesses, whether it's a minor adjustment or major overhaul, and effectively deliver these improvements.

The first step is to establish a focus for your customer satisfaction efforts. This task, critical in determining the scope and benefits from your subsequent efforts, is detailed in the Preliminary Step of the program outlined in Chapter 8. This procedure guides you to an objective through the use of a simple customer feedback exercise. The goal will be to select the area that has the biggest potential for improving customer satisfaction.

After deciding on an objective, select a name for your program. Call it whatever you like. For example, if your interest is to improve response time to customers, call the program, "The Customer Connection: Swift and Superior Service." This clearly states the objective of the program. If the purpose is to motivate employees within your customer service department, try, "Customer Satisfaction: Our Business." Almost any name will do—but make sure it specifically identifies the objective. Create a name that conveys knowledge ("Customer Satisfaction: Our Business"), enthusiasm (*our* business), and a focus for the program (*swift* service).

Disney chairman Michael Eisner established the Disney "Vision of Quality Service." This theme is an important part of employees' orientation and despite its lack of detail (a better title might be "Disney Vision of Excellence—Quality, Service, and Smiles"), it effectively carries its message to all Disney "cast members." This service philosophy is an essential part of standard operating procedure and basic management policy, empowering Disney cast members and helping to measure service performance and maintain the highest standards of design and construction in the Walt Disney World manufacturing area. This basic management policy is communicated throughout the organization and has become a practical and cost-justified corporate strategy.

---

 *P*ick a name for your customer satisfaction program. Include your objective within the name. Make it accurate, simple, and exciting.

Identify with the Customer

One way to appreciate the customer perspective is to examine the customer experience with your products and services. This is commonly known as the *customer service cycle* and has two parts: The customer side and the service side. The customer side traces the customer experience in obtaining products and services. The service side identifies the production steps involved in servicing customers (those steps necessary to support the customer side). We will evaluate both sides of the cycle and then apply a method to improve the entire process.

To construct the customer side, think of one product or service that you or others in your organization may be concerned about. (You will complete this in detail in Step 1 of the World-Class Customer Satisfaction Program.) This could be your main source of business (e.g., lodging for business travelers), or it could be a problem area that is a constant drain on resources (lodging for bus tour groups). Perhaps it has recently been the subject of complaints and needs improvement. Take the customer perspective, starting with the first contact with your organization (with products, advertisements, or whatever). Move through the consumption experience and conclude with any after-purchase contact.

A customer cycle identifies the stages of a customer's typical experience with a firm's products and services. For example, the customer cycle for a hotel guest would include: reservations, arrival, registration, telephone operator, room service, restaurant (formal or informal), checkout and departure.

To construct the service side of the customer service cycle, think of what it takes to deliver products and services to customers. Include everything that supports the steps on the customer side. Remember, this is not the customer's experience—this is the firm's experience. Even if these are already printed in the form of operating procedures, often called *standards of performance* or *quality standards*, enter the descriptions as part of the cycle.

The service cycle that corresponds to the first step in the (above) customer cycle would include:

Reservations: Answer phone before fourth ring with hotel greeting. Offer assistance. Write down critical customer information. Make suggestions. Use client's name. Confirm requests. Follow up with letter and appropriate materials.

Each step in the service cycle requires at least this level of detail. Take a moment to sketch out, or think about, the customer side and service side of a customer service cycle in your organization. Select either a precise customer experience to outline or use a more general customer experience. Remember, you will have an opportunity to focus on this cycle in the program at the end of the book.

Internal Partnering

Once you've decided on the name and focus of your program, ask one of your managers for support, preferably your superior. This is critical, as nothing does more to transform a company than an initial push by management and a continuing leadership vision.

Seek out the support from one manager above you or another strong advocate.

Explain your interest in improving customer satisfaction. Tell him or her that customer satisfaction and loyalty efforts will cost little compared to their tremendous profit potential. For ammunition use examples of companies profiting directly from improved customer satisfaction (use the companies listed in Exhibit 1–1). Even if the manager only responds with simple verbal acknowledgment, this communication will help to encourage your efforts from the start. Write a note to the manager to acknowledge and thank him or her for the support. You could pick a colleague from another department who is well respected and would serve as a key advocate. Or pick someone who might otherwise obstruct your efforts. The more the merrier, but simply finding a supporting colleague can be very helpful.

The Executive Partner

Everybody can't work directly with a senior manager. Upper management may be useful for getting the program running, but its destiny will be determined by those employees who deal directly with customers. You will, however, be responsible for defending and communicating the value of your program right from the start. Very few companies offer great customer satisfaction mainly because many of its basic principles are misunderstood. Knowing these principles, which are noted every few pages with a globe, can take you through the turbulent waters of change. Applying these concepts, after formulating a well-stated objective, can simplify the approach to improving customer satisfaction and help gain the support of others more readily.

Internal barriers prevent companies from delivering satisfaction. For many firms, it takes years for their entire organization to begin to demonstrate a customer focus. It's difficult for employees to stay committed to a customer focus when the chief executive and the managers themselves are not dedicated to customer needs. For example, what kind of message do managers send workers if they tout "customer name recognition" as critical to providing good customer service, yet don't even know the names of their employees? On the other hand, think of the tone managers could set in an organization by making it a point to warmly greet all employees by name.

> *M*anagement should set the pace by demonstrating how to deliver internal and external customer satisfaction. Each activity should be personally executed with as much, or more, detail and follow-through than is expected of others.

Leaders often lose their commitment by refocusing on research and development, engineering, and budgeting issues. Without proper leadership, effective customer-oriented programs don't stand a chance and more mundane operational issues that can be barriers to customer satisfaction will quickly take precedence.

As a result of such impatience, executive decisions are often sweeping and tend toward uniformity. "We want a complete customer satisfaction program by next week!" the company chairman announces. Initial interest by top management is no guarantee of success. Customer satisfaction efforts can represent a dramatic change in the way decisions are made and require innovation as well as attention to detail. Customer satisfaction is won one customer at a time. Generalized approaches typically create rigid control at the expense of flexibility.

At The Ritz-Carlton Hotel Company, top executives form the senior quality committee. This group initiated the strategies and served on the application team that led to their Malcolm Baldrige National Quality Award in 1992. This team continues to meet weekly to review standards and performance and evaluate indicators of guest satisfaction, market growth, development, profit, and competitive status. By dedicating two to three days per week to these guest-oriented programs, these senior managers avoid being immersed in mundane activities and losing their customer commitment.

Between 1988 and 1994, 19 companies won the Malcolm Baldrige National Quality Award. The companies are listed in Exhibit 1–3. The award is based on seven categories:

- Methods for assuring quality goods and services.
- Information and analysis.
- Leadership.
- Strategic quality planning.

EXHIBIT 1–3
Benchmarking the Baldrige Winners

Year	Manufacturing	Small Business	Service Companies
1988	Motorola Inc.	Globe Metallurgical Inc.	
	Commercial Nuclear Fuel, Division of Westinghouse		
1989	Milliken & Co.		
	Xerox Corp. Business Products and Systems		
1990	Cadillac Motor Car Div.	Wallace Co. Inc.	Federal Express Corporation
	IBM Rochester		
1991	Solectron Corp	Marlow Industries	
	Zytec Corp.		
1992	AT&T Network Systems, Transmission Systems	Granite Rock Co.	AT&T Universal Card Services
	Texas Instruments Inc., Defense Systems & Electronics Group		The Ritz-Carlton Hotel Co.
1993	Eastman Chemical	Ames Rubber Corp.	

- Human resource development and management.
- Quality and operational results.
- Customer focus and satisfaction.

Individual copies of the application guidelines are available free of charge from: Malcolm Baldrige National Quality Award, National Institute of Standards and Technology, Route 270 and Quince Orchard Road, Administration Building, Room A537, Gaithersburg, MD, 20899, (301) 975-2036, fax (301) 948-3716.

As the president of a Baldrige winning company put it, "When senior leaders personally instill a strong vision and a set of principles in their employees and then give them the confidence, freedom, and authority to act, people take responsibility for their jobs and do whatever is necessary to satisfy their customers."[9] Even if not initiated by senior management, the ultimate success of any serious customer satisfaction effort will need the explicit support of its leadership.

 Senior managers should know about customer satisfaction efforts even if they're not directly involved; and they should demonstrate the same commitment they expect from their employees.

For a business to be successful in the long run, it must satisfy customers at a profit. Colleagues, management, customers, and even your competition will help you to achieve this. As Peter Drucker said, "The only valid . . . business purpose is to create a satisfied customer." Customer satisfaction serves as an appropriate company objective to hold its various functions together and direct corporate resources. All company activities, programs, and policies should be evaluated in terms of their contribution to satisfying customers—apart from their contribution to other company objectives.

SUMMARY

- World-class companies have broadened and accelerated their efforts toward improvement by making significant advances in product and service quality, employee training, and other customer treatment areas.
- World-class companies understand what satisfies their clientele the most and utilize this information in customer programs and employee training to promote customer loyalty.
- Service is only part of what it takes to satisfy customers. Good service does not guarantee satisfaction.
- Companies known for customer satisfaction outperform others in their industry.
- An internal customer is the employee who receives and uses output from another person or area. The internal customer concept means treating internal customers with a similar level of respect and attention that external customers receive.
- Pick a name for your customer satisfaction program. Include your objective within the name. Make it accurate, simple, and exciting.

- Seek out the support from one manager above you or another strong advocate.
- Management should personally set the pace by demonstrating how to deliver internal and external customer satisfaction. Each activity should be personally executed with as much, or more, detail and follow-through than is expected of others.
- Senior managers should know about customer satisfaction efforts even if they're not directly involved; and they should demonstrate the same commitment they expect from their employees.

NOTES

1. John Ryan, "1987 ASQC/Gallup Survey" *Quality Progress* 20, no. 12, December 87, pp. 12–17.
2. Arild Lillebo, "Serving Tomorrow's Needs," *Profile*, August 1983.
3. Robert A. Westbrook, J. Newman, and J. Taylor, "Satisfaction/Dissatisfaction in the Purchase Decision Process," *Journal of Marketing* 42 (October 1978): p. 59.
4. G. Lynn Shostack, "Designing Services That Deliver," *Harvard Business Review*, January–February, 1984, pp. 133–139.
5. Richard Gibson, "Waiter, I'd Like Another Waiter," *The Wall Street Journal*," July 14, 1993, p. B1.
6. From a speech given by Richard Rosenburg, CEO, Bank of America. Hilton Hotel, San Francisco, March 15, 1993.
7. Adapted from "Customer Service Impacts Cash Flow," *Supervision*, June 1993, pp. 8–9.
8. Churchill and Surprenant, "An Investigation into the Determinants of Customer Satisfaction," *Journal of Marketing Research* 19 (November 1982), pp. 491–504.
9. Horst Schultze, president, The Ritz-Carlton Hotel Company. From the company's Malcolm Baldrige National Quality Award application summary, 1992, p. 4.

Chapter Two

The Ingredients of Customer Satisfaction

Exceeding Expectations, Delivering Quality, and Targeting Customer Preferences

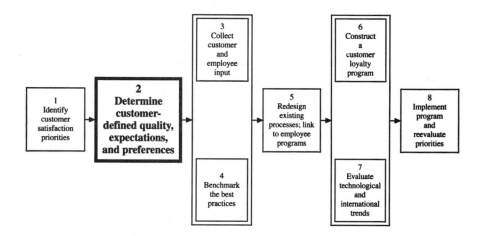

There's never a good sale *for the store unless it's a good* buy *for the customer.*

Stanley Marcus, *Minding the Store.*

This chapter presents a new definition and understanding of customer satisfaction. It discusses customer expectations, the quality of the customer experience, and customer preferences.

CUSTOMER EXPECTATIONS

Why did the 1993 presidential inauguration cost $25 million? Bill Clinton wanted his inauguration and especially the inaugural address to have a big impact, clearing the way for the ideas he was promoting. He used the power of his position and the mood of the country to create an atmosphere for change. Although he would not personally be involved in most of what was to be accomplished, his intent was to advance and capitalize on the expectations of the country.

Clinton's inauguration was followed by big expectations, but in his first year he earned low ratings in the polls. In addition to pressing economic, international, and social problems, he faced the high hurdle of meeting the raised expectations of the American public. People were looking for a quick fix, which was impossible because of the complexity and gravity of the problems.

During his first State of the Union address in January 1994, Clinton reassured the American public that he had not forgotten the promises he made in his campaign and in his inaugural address. He also emphasized his programs to address the concerns of the American people about crime, state of the family, and welfare reform. This speech resulted in a significant upturn in the polls. Clinton not only overcame the problem of unrealized expectations but also responded to the changing concerns of his public.

Expectations are what people think is likely to occur in the future. We form expectations, for example, when we hope, anticipate, or dread. Looking forward to seeing a friend, waiting for a favorite TV show, or fearing the dentist are reactions based on expectations. In each case, we compare our perceptions of the new experience with previous experiences, feelings, or other information gathered from a variety of sources.

In 1993 leading hotel company presidents made various claims for their companies: "We provide total customer satisfaction!" "We will be the leading global hospitality group by consistently exceeding customers expectations through innovation and quality" "We're committed to 100 percent customer satisfaction."

Many companies, like politicians, are unable to live up to strong claims. Known as *lip-service*, or overstating capabilities and delivering less than promised, these exaggerated claims can undermine the credibility and efforts of persons and organizations that, in reality, are providing superior products and service. The perception of superior performance can be eroded when preceded by exaggerated promises. Overzealous claims not

EXHIBIT 2-1
Customer Expectation Model

Company-Controlled Expectation Creators	+	Uncontrollable Expectation Creators	—>	Customers' Standards
Product experience		Competitors		Ideal
Short- and long-term marketing strategies		Preferences		Predicted
		Word of mouth		Minimum

only disappoint customers but result in big losses for companies whose programs don't deliver. Insupportable claims can be more damaging than claiming nothing at all. Even nonverbal communication, such as, advertising designs, signage, logos, or the appearance of public entrances, can create very specific expectations for a firm's products and services.

Companies are responsible for the expectations they create. They should know how their products, services, promotions, personnel, facilities, reputation, and so forth affect customers. They should be aware of what their competition is known for and how customers weigh this information. This process—how expectations are created and formed into standards by which an organization's performance is measured—can be a valuable planning tool for management (Exhibit 2-1).

If your company says its purpose is to serve the customer, its hours must be convenient, prices reasonable, and staff helpful and courteous. But if the company doesn't meet its claims (e.g., cuts its hours), customers quickly become skeptical and dissatisfied. However, by not making claims—no promises, pledges, assurances, and so on, either verbally or nonverbally the company focuses less attention on specific products and services and creates lower customer expectations.

Customers are exposed to many clues that give information about individual products and services. By connecting brand name, product quality, and the personal treatment received, with previous associations, customers form opinions, make judgments, and redefine expectations. These expectations, like first impressions, are easily created and may last a long time. This is why knowing what creates initial expectations or what can affect expectations over time is so important for companies. More significant or deliberate steps, such as innovations and long-term marketing strategies, are necessary to affect established customer attitudes.

*C*ustomers use the information provided about your products and services to form expectations.

Imagine walking into a restaurant and observing an elegant, cathedral-sized dining area, marble floors, white stone pillars, and the sounds of classical music. When the Sheraton Palace Hotel in San Francisco completed its $180 million face-lift, their historic, grand entrance presented this scene. The previously lackluster appearance was transformed into a truly magnificent room and striking hotel entrance. Baroque music, exotic plants, stained glass windows, and prize sculptures created a peaceful, time-honored impression.

Most of the new hotels built in downtown San Francisco within the last five years have been luxury properties, and the public assumed this to be another. But when guests strolled into the new Sheraton Palace Hotel, sat down and ordered coffee, the service was more akin to a three-star restaurant. Quick-tempered, poorly dressed servers were too busy for the swelling numbers of customers. The hotel's opening publicity efforts had helped make this room a favorite media spot—tourists, guests, and sightseers all converged to experience this remade historical landmark. But as the dust settled and only the regular paying customers remained, the poor service stood out. It was certainly not the five-star level suggested by the elegance of the hotel entrance and lobby.

Sheraton never intended this to be a first-class hotel. Guests were paying rates much lower than those charged at the nearby luxury hotels. The management was, however, forced to upgrade the service in the lobby and restaurant to approximate the level that was suggested by the surroundings. Expectations can be powerful.

 *T*he perception of superior performance can be eroded when preceded by exaggerated promises.

But what do customers expect? The key to this question is the word *customers*. This means current customers, not lost or future customers. These current customers have chosen to do business with you today. The trick is to identify why. Specifically, what did customers expect when they chose to come to you? For example, if a Mexican restaurant offers only selec-

EXHIBIT 2–2
Continuum of Expectation Creators

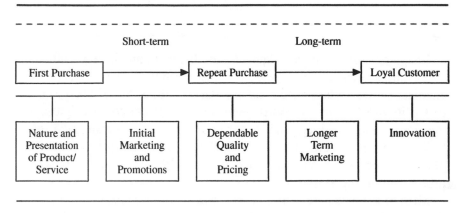

tions from a ceviche bar (serving only raw, marinated fish), customers will likely be dissatisfied. They probably expected more familiar fare like burritos and enchiladas. This type of disappointment can be prevented by obtaining regular customer feedback.

Controlling customer expectations is a major challenge to management. Let's first examine the two ways customer expectations are created: through company-controlled efforts, and by other uncontrollable elements. Then we'll look at the customer standards these create.

Company-Controlled Expectation Creators: Product Experience, Short- and Long-Term Marketing Strategies

Organizations can affect customer expectations by understanding how the company's actions contribute to their creation. By knowing what it is about products and services, advertising, pricing policies, reputation, and service quality that is most significant to and remembered by customers, companies can coordinate these elements to create or modify expectations.

Expectation creators can be short- or long-term, as shown on the continuum presented in Exhibit 2–2. Short-term expectation creators include:

1. Nature and presentation of products and services.
2. Advertising and promotions.

3. Store-front and signage (packaging).
4. Image, decor, ambience, and status.
5. First impressions of employees and other customers.
6. In-store merchandising.

Long-term expectation creators include:

1. Consistent delivery and quality of products and services.
2. Innovation in products and services (changing menu, decor).
3. Marketing efforts (advertising and promotions).
4. Pricing policy variations (value over time).

Each of these components can represent tangible aspects of your organization's products and services that can be manipulated to affect customer expectations. The key is to review what these components are for your organization and understand how they effect customers expectations.

Uncontrollable Expectation Creators: Competitors, Preferences, Word of Mouth

A company can't control all the elements that help create customer expectations about its products and services. Competitors' advertising and pricing practices can affect how customers see your products and services. Customers' experiences with competing products and services also influence their expectations of your organization. Individual customer preferences (favorite colors, personal opinions, tastes, and so on) and word-of-mouth information can also make independent contributions to customer expectations. The key is to try to maintain awareness of these uncontrollable influences and to incorporate this information into your efforts to manage the controllable expectation creators.

Creating Standards: Ideal, Predicted, Minimum

The disconfirmation paradigm maintains that customers compare a new product or service experience with some standard (expectation) they have developed.[1]

These standards are not specific points in the customer's head. Instead, ideal, predicted, and minimum expectations represent a range of outcomes that customers anticipate on the basis of all the information they have accumulated. Customers use this as a frame of reference when they assess their entire product or service experience.

Ideal. This expectation, based partly on experience and partly on desire, is the level a customer hopes to receive. An example of an ideal expectation is, "I was there a long time ago, but from what I remember, this was my favorite."

Predicted. This standard is based on a customer's experience with the product or with similar, competitive products. It represents what is most likely to occur. For example, a customer may say, "Look, I've been to their stores in Frankfurt, Paris, and Johannesburg, and McDonald's french fries can't be beat!"

Minimum. This level will be acceptable but contributes to minimal satisfaction. For example, "Well dear, even if it's not the greatest, let's stay there anyway—at least it's clean."

Companies can find out if they met expectations simply by asking customers, "Did we meet your expectations?" AT&T won two Malcolm Baldrige National Quality Awards in 1992 by focusing on customer expectations. They identified what their customers expect: performance, reliability, competitive price, responsiveness, specific features, on-time delivery, service, and a clear and correct bill (see Step 2a in Chapter 8 for identifying what your customers expect). AT&T recognized that customers buy products and services that deliver what is expected. They also realized that what is expected is a moving target, driven by fast-paced technology and the achievements of best-in-class performers in all industries. AT&T confronted these circumstances by focusing on its employees (strong empowerment programs give frontline staff enough flexibility, and therefore incentive, to please customers) and by knowing their customers (customer programs center on collecting feedback from customers and examining and guiding improvement efforts.)

Customers form their expectations by storing this new information according to its source (experience, preference, word of mouth, or competitor). Customers can easily call on this information to evaluate a situation, at least in part. Customers evaluate the situation using a range of benchmarks, comparing the new information to their ideal, predicted, or minimum levels. For example, the range of standards for expectations about automobiles may be:

- Ideal: The perfect car, a Red Jaguar (uncontrollable).
- Predicted: Experience with cars, Hondas (controllable).
- Minimum: Experiences with similar brands, other Japanese small cars (uncontrollable).

These benchmarks help customers to develop their own expectations of any product or service. The key is to review how these levels (ideal, predicted, and minimum) apply to your organization and to incorporate this information into your efforts to manage the controllable expectation creators.

For example, a customer may predict a high value in a Honda on the basis of what he has heard or been exposed to from formal marketing efforts. Or, because of his experience with Honda motorcycles, he expects good value in a Honda automobile. If Honda found that enough customers have similar perceptions, the company could develop hard-hitting advertisements focusing on the value of their cars (resale value, low maintenance, and so forth) versus that of the competition. Reference to their well-known motorcycles could also reinforce their tradition of value.

*F*ocus on improving areas where customer expectations are low and the value, or importance, to customers is high.

Setting Expectation Levels

Pretend you just returned from lunch at McDonald's with a friend. There were about twice as many people working behind the counter as there were waiting in line. When you were served, you felt you were treated personally rather than like part of a mass production process. The food was what you expected, the same as on your last visit. Tables, floors, and bathrooms were clean. Altogether it was a good experience.

Now, imagine you and your friend visited a new French restaurant. Upon entering you saw many waiters dressed in tuxedos moving about a full dining room. There were chandeliers, white tablecloths, candles, and so forth. You and your friend waited nearly 25 minutes at the bar and didn't feel very welcome. After you were finally seated near the kitchen, your waiter Paul appeared, took a deep breath, and recited a litany of specials. The second or third one sounded interesting, but not wanting to review them, you picked the last one you remembered. The meal was average—but it was nice to eat French for a change. Your conversation was interesting, so you had dessert and coffee. Paul immediately delivered the bill and you paid it, although with some hesitation.

The actual delivery of service is critical to forming expectations. How can McDonald's provide excellent service with few employees, and why does an expensive restaurant with a huge staff have a harder time? Different expectations. Differing levels of expectations explain why a company offering more service can end up doing worse than a company offering less service. Setting customer expectations at the right level is the key. And it's tough to do. Waiting in line at a bank for four minutes will please a customer who expected it to take five minutes but disappoint one who anticipated a wait of two minutes.

Service Wars
An electronic queuing system called Camtron measures the time a bank customer waits on line and displays it for both customers and employees to see. It automatically routes customers to the next available teller via a flashing light. The system also projects staffing requirements.[2]

Microsoft employs two full-time "hold-jockeys" to oversee the customers who are on hold, waiting to talk with a technical support person. Customers initially input the type of problem they're experiencing and receive personalized messages about how much longer they have to wait. This is possible because of software that tracks the status of all callers and allows the two hold-jockeys to estimate when a call will be answered.

If expectations about a product or service get too high, the organization becomes vulnerable to customer dissatisfaction. If your expectations for the French restaurant, for example, were reduced by its modest prices, then you may not have been as disappointed with the experience. But by creating lofty expectations, the French restaurant was doomed to fail. It created expectations beyond its own performance abilities.

---

*E*xpectation levels should be set high enough to attract business but accurate enough to reflect the reality of what is likely to be delivered 100 percent of the time.

According to Sylvester Stallone, part owner of Planet Hollywood, a restaurant chain with locations worldwide, the restaurant is so popular because it delivers more than people expected. The walls are covered with movie star memorabilia, and co-owners Bruce Willis and Arnold Schwarzenegger along with Sylvester Stallone can sometimes be found running around serving great food. People are stunned.

Rising Expectations

Nothing is as good as it seems beforehand.

George Eliot, Silas Marner (1861).

The best part of our lives we pass in counting on what is to come.

William Hazlitt, "On Novelty and Familiarity," *The Plain Speaker* (1826)

These quotes portray our enthusiastic tendency to embellish the future, a habit that makes a company's task of meeting expectations increasingly difficult.

A study of hotel guests found that repeat customers (guests who had visited the hotel at least once before) were less satisfied than first-time customers. One explanation may be that the repeat guests return for a purpose different from their previous visit and, therefore, bring different expectations. A second, and more likely, explanation may be that return customers tend to have heightened expectations of familiar products or services. Just as movie sequels tend to be disappointing and often let down viewers, a return visit to a hotel may lack the freshness and originality of the initial stay. These new customer expectations can't be met in the same way as they were in the previous experience. Increasing expectations is a logical and accepted phenomenon.

 *C*ustomer expectations will increase—so should your ability to meet and exceed them.

The vision statement for Residence Inns by Marriott begins with "Residence Inn will exceed the expectations of every guest, every day, every stay." This creates a demanding standard to constantly improve performance and a considerable responsibility for each employee to meet. Yet

Residence Inns has led its market since Marriott purchased the chain in 1987.

Companies need to constantly improve the performance of products and services to survive in a growing economy. Customers, therefore, learn to anticipate and demand these improvements. So how do we handle this phenomenon? Continuous improvement. Improve quality to meet rising levels of customer expectations. Continuous improvement means refinement and innovation to affect customer satisfaction. Marriott, for example, commits their organization to "constantly improve our systems, practices and capabilities . . . "[3] We will consider how to accomplish this in the section on quality later in this chapter.

Give Customers What They Don't Expect

Meeting expectations is only the minimum requirement for a successful customer satisfaction strategy. Surpassing expectations is the key to customer satisfaction. Perpetually raising product and service quality, however, is not the only way to exceed expectations. Although the focus should be on continuous improvement, one way to exceed customer expectations is through surprise—dazzle customers with something out of the blue rather than with small changes to the familiar. A recent government survey, "What the Customer Wants," found that most adults enjoy the unexpected and search for novelty, excitement, and immediate gratification.

 Surprise is one way to exceed customer expectations. Promise what to expect, deliver this or more, and sometimes surprise customers.

Hotels have caught onto this idea. Some innovative hotels have gone beyond providing amenities to impress guests. A Marriott Hotel in Miami already offers environmentally correct guest rooms, "green rooms" that include special air and water filtration, water-conserving faucets, and energy-efficient light bulbs. It has also installed a $12,000 machine that releases floral and citrus natural plant abstracts into the lobby through the central air conditioner. The desired effect of this aromatherapy is to reduce stress and was tailored to the hotel's Central and South American guests.

The ability to control and affect expectations certainly would be a powerful tool in the quest to satisfy customers. Managers may accomplish this, in part, by identifying the elements of customer expectations that they can control. By focusing on these areas and measuring the impact of those efforts over time (using a variety of customer feedback techniques, Exhibit 3–1), managers can begin to understand how they can directly affect customer expectations.

This valuable information can be used in planning and development, an area in which U.S. firms lag behind German and Japanese competitors. One study found that 58 percent of Japanese firms use customer expectation data in their product design; 40 percent of German firms do; but only 22 percent of U.S. firms reported using this important information.

Maintaining high levels of customer satisfaction requires companies to continually exceed expectations, especially in areas most affecting customers. Communicate what is likely to occur, provide at least this level, and sometimes surprise customers.

QUALITY

Quality is a journey not a destination.[4]
Quality is remembered long after price is forgotten.

What do Ritz-Carlton, Buick, Ford,[5] Xerox, Federal Express, Milliken, 3M, Motorola, Apple, Hewlett-Packard, and many Fortune 500 companies have in common? Each has made a companywide commitment to pursue the obscure goal of *quality*. The reason is that Americans are willing to pay a premium for quality. A 1992 Gallup survey found that shoppers would pay 72 percent above the base price of a sofa for a better piece of furniture; 67 percent more than the base price for a high tech TV; 42 percent above the $400 base price of a new dishwasher, and 21 percent above $12,000 sticker price for a late model car. Customers still believe that price is an indicator of quality. Buying well-made imports for more than a decade has also educated consumers.

 Americans are attracted to excellence and are willing to pay extra for quality.

In 1988 the U.S. Department of Commerce initiated the Malcolm Baldrige National Quality Award to recognize American companies that were doing an exceptional job of providing quality products and services to their customers (refer to Exhibit 1–3). Since then hundreds of companies have applied for this award, and the winners have increased its public awareness and prestige by highlighting it in their marketing efforts.

Quality Is No Longer Job One

Ford Motor Company has shifted its focus from quality to customer satisfaction.

Ford has developed an aggressive new customer satisfaction program to improve customer treatment—from the salesperson's showroom greeting to the service and maintenance department's speed and quality of workmanship. Their strategy for building customer satisfaction includes three elements:

Quality (lower left of figure) is now recognized as a part of customer satisfaction. Ford believes that as a result of its "Quality Is Job One" ad campaign, they are already established as the quality leader, and the shift in focus to the "Customer Is Job One" satisfaction program will complement this status.

Why all this attention on improving quality now? According to Robert Stempel, recently retired president of General Motors, "not too long ago . . . quality meant that you were expected to have a certain number of

EXHIBIT 2-3
Producer versus Customer Logic

Producers	Customers
Think they are making products.	Think they are buying services.
Worry about visible mistakes.	Worry about invisible mistakes.
Think technologies create products.	Think desires create products.
Organize for managerial convenience.	Want their convenience to come first.
Seek a high level of productivity.	Seek a high standard of living.

Source: Based on Rosabeth Moss Canter, *Harvard Business Review*, July–August 1992, p. 9–10.

defects." Stemple knows, however, that GM's "certain number of defects" cost them a lot of sales, and multiple problems resulted in more customer dissatisfaction and lower repurchase intentions.

International competition has challenged us to improve product and service quality. In overall demand for products, Japan still sells more to U.S. consumers than our own domestic companies. In customer evaluations of automobile quality, Japanese and German cars are rated superior to American cars.

Why can't Americans get it together to produce higher-quality products and services? According to a 1990 poll, American producers define quality as the measure of how close their products meet predetermined specifications. They emphasize techniques of product, planning, design, production, and control to achieve product quality. Customers, on the other hand, define quality as how well their needs are met and emphasize a product's reliability, durability, ease of use, and low price.

Producers are not focusing on the customer definition of quality. Their view of quality does not emphasize customer satisfaction. Product specifications should be identified not only for production but also for use. This separation of product production and product use is the root of the quality problem in this country (Exhibit 2–3).

Your product isn't reliable unless the customer says it's reliable. Your service isn't fast unless the customer says it's fast. If your customer says that the lighting in the room is improper, you may be tempted to defend the current setup by responding with details about the size of the room, the angle of the sun, energy, wiring considerations, and so on. But if the guest says it's unacceptable, it is.

Managers themselves can attempt to define quality from the customer's perspective. For example, key managers of the organization can brainstorm the attributes of quality associated with their products and services. One session can yield 100 or more attributes that the participants condense into 10 to 12 major attributes. It can also help to discuss these attributes with managers from other departments (and, ideally, with their customers) before adopting a final set of attributes on which the company focuses marketing efforts.

 *M*anagement may estimate quality standards, but customers have to refine them. These standards should include both production and use components.

Service Quality

No company can possibly cover every customer interaction within a job description or other formal documentation. But each customer interaction should be planned by considering the process and desired outcomes of these interactions. Service quality has been interpreted to include five dimensions: R   A   T   E   R.[6]

On the basis of your customer service cycle (Chapter 1), consider how each of these dimensions can be applied to each customer interface. Please refer to Step 2b in Chapter 8 to complete this in detail.

The numbers in parentheses indicate the relative importance of these dimensions according to a recent study of 1,900 customers of five different service companies.[7]

Reliability:	Dependability and correctness. (32)
Assurance:	Knowledge and courtesy of employees. (22)
Tangibles:	Appearance of physical facilities, equipment, and personnel. (19)
Empathy:	Providing personal understanding and customer support. (16)
Responsiveness:	Providing prompt service. (11)

Quality standards are important to ensure consistent levels of performance. In manufacturing beer, Heineken requires that the head in a poured glass of beer last for five minutes. It will reject any batch of beer that misses this mark by 20 seconds. This quality standard was identified through customer input. Similarly, quality service standards can be developed using customer input for each step of the customer service cycle. These standards should address the five RATER dimensions of service quality and should consider customer expectations.

For example, let's look at the customer service cycle for room service. Applying these five dimensions of quality to only step one of this cycle might look like this:

Room Service Guest Service Cycle

Step 1: Guest Calls Room Service

Quality Dimensions	Quality Service Standards
Reliability	Phone answered within five rings, 24 hours a day.
Assurance	Phone operator has thorough knowledge of menu and prices.
Tangibles	Full description of items and presentation. Specific delivery time stated.
Empathy	Customer name used. Prescribed guest treatment procedure carried out with sincerity. Order taken in courteous manner.
Responsiveness	Effort to comply with any special requests. Prompt service.

The purpose of assigning quality standards to each step of customer service cycles is to promote consistency and superior performance. Quality standards provide direction and motivation for employees. Superior performance is more likely achieved when quality standards are clearly communicated and when they are connected to employees' performance/appraisal/reward system (Chapter 5). Once established, these standards should be evaluated on a regular basis and provide a systematic means to assess service performance (see Exhibit 2–4).

Ritz-Carlton Hotels developed its own standards for quality service. Known as *Gold Standards*, these are four tools that help define the beliefs and behaviors of their quality service concept (See Exhibit 2–5). These include the company's "Three Steps of Service," "Motto," "Credo," and "Basics of Service," statements. These standards, printed on pocket cards, are intended for use at all levels of their organization and were the principal customer tools that contributed to Ritz-Carlton winning the 1992 Malcolm Baldrige National Quality Award.

EXHIBIT 2–4
Service Standards Evaluation

HILTON
STANDARDS OF PRODUCT AND PERFORMANCE

Front Desk   **Check-Out**

Day/Date: _____   **Check-Out GSA:** _____

Dispute: _____   **Time:** _____

Criteria	Yes	No	N/A	Comment
1. Check-out line and transaction time do not exceed 10 minutes (unless customer requires and asks for additional assistance).	___	___	___	___
2. GSA offers guest a review of his/her charges and determines if any additional ones are not noted.	___	___	___	___
3. GSA asks about guest's satisfaction.	___	___	___	___
4. GSA thanks guest for staying with hotel and invites him/her to return.	___	___	___	___
5. Guest last name used during check-out	___	___	___	___

Total Points Achieved: ___

Total Points Possible: ___

% Achieved: ___

Source: Reprinted with the permission of Hilton Hotels Corporation.

EXHIBIT 2-5
The Ritz-Carlton's Customer Tools

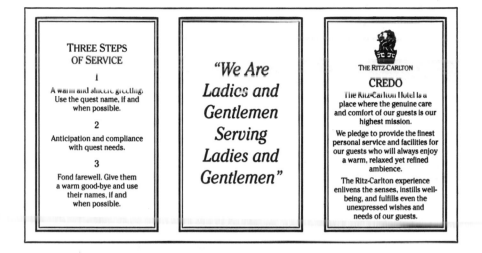

THREE STEPS
OF SERVICE

1

A warm and sincere greeting.
Use the guest name, if and
when possible.

2

Anticipation and compliance
with guest needs.

3

Fond farewell. Give them
a warm good-bye and use
their names, if and
when possible.

"We Are Ladies and Gentlemen Serving Ladies and Gentlemen"

THE RITZ-CARLTON

CREDO

The Ritz-Carlton Hotel is a
place where the genuine care
and comfort of our guests is our
highest mission.

We pledge to provide the finest
personal service and facilities for
our guests who will always enjoy
a warm, relaxed yet refined
ambience.

The Ritz-Carlton experience
enlivens the senses, instills well-
being, and fulfills even the
unexpressed wishes and
needs of our guests.

THE RITZ-CARLTON BASICS

1 The Credo will be known, owned and energized by all employees.
2 Our motto is: "We are Ladies and Gentlemen serving Ladies and Gentlemen". Practice teamwork and "lateral service" to create a positive work environment.
3 The three steps of service shall be practiced by all employees.
4 All employees will successfully complete Training Certification to ensure they understand how to perform to The Ritz-Carlton standards in their position.
5 Each employee will understand their work area and Hotel goals as established in each strategic plan.
6 All employees will know the needs of their internal and external customers (guests and employees) so that we may deliver the products and services they expect. Use guest preference pads to record specific needs.
7 Each employee will continuously identify defects (Mr. BIV) throughout the Hotel.

8 Any employee who receives a customer complaint "owns" the complaint.
9 Instant guest pacification will be ensured by all. React quickly to correct the problem immediately. Follow-up with a telephone call within twenty minutes to verify the problem has been resolved to the customer's satisfaction. Do everything you possibly can to never lose a guest.
10 Guest incident action forms are used to record and communicate every incident of guest dissatisfaction. Every employee is empowered to resolve the problem and to prevent a repeat occurrence.
11 Uncompromising levels of cleanliness are the responsibility of every employee.
12 "Smile – We are on stage." Always maintain positive eye contact. Use the proper vocabulary with our guests. (Use words like – "Good Morning," "Certainly," "I'll be happy to" and "My pleasure").
13 Be an ambassador of your Hotel in and outside of the work place. Always talk positively. No negative comments.
14 Escort guests rather than pointing out directions to another area of the Hotel.
15 Be knowledgeable of Hotel information (hours of operation, etc.) to answer guest

inquiries. Always recommend the Hotel's retail and food and beverage outlets prior to outside facilities.
16 Use proper telephone etiquette. Answer within three rings and with a "smile." When necessary, ask the caller, "May I place you on hold." Do not screen calls. Eliminate call transfers when possible.
17 Uniforms are to be immaculate; Wear proper and safe footware (clean and polished), and your correct name tag. Take pride and care in your personal appearance (adhering to all grooming standards).
18 Ensure all employees know their roles during emergency situations and are aware of fire and life safety response processes.
19 Notify your supervisor immediately of hazards, injuries, equipment or assistance that you need. Practice energy conservation and proper maintenance and repair of Hotel property and equipment.
20 Protecting the assets of a Ritz-Carlton Hotel is the responsibility of every employee

1092

What Is Total Quality Management?

Total quality management (TQM) is a philosophy that emphasizes quality measurement through statistical process control, and group problem-solving efforts such as quality circles (see Exhibit 2–6). It is based on the

EXHIBIT 2–6
The Total Quality Management (TQM) Process

1. Specify current performance standards.
2. Identify where outputs are at variance with standards.
3. Determine the cause of the variance.
4. Identify and initiate actions to correct causes of variance.
5. Specify desired performance.
6. Compare the desired standards to current standards and identify gaps.
7. Develop alternatives to close the gaps.
8. Institutionalize new standards.

Source: Shaun P. McCormack, "TQM: Getting It Right the First Time," *Training and Development*, June 1992, p. 45.

idea of continuous improvement and centers on top management support, employee involvement, the internal customer concept, process improvement, and recognition rewards. All of these major components are included within the World-Class Customer Satisfaction Program in Chapter 8. TQM is also useful, as an excellent tool for control. For this purpose, we will consider what TQM offers as a tool for maintaining quality standards.

Despite the limitations of TQM, many organizations are using some form of it in an attempt to overcome their insensitivity to customers. It is being applied to all functions of the organization, from human resource management to long-term planning. The challenge of the TQM concept is to continually define and improve customer-perceived quality. Organizations must identify what product and service quality means to customers. This quality identification task can be supported with the latest techniques of total quality management such as statistical process control (SPC), quality function deployment (QFD) and statistical quality control (SQC) methods. Exhibit 2–7 describes some of the techniques of SPC.

Statistical process control is one of the most important advances in quality management. This approach to quality control allows management to oversee the service delivery process instead of relying on a final inspection, defect count, or worse, hearing complaints directly from customers.

The basic techniques of SPC can be used by nonspecialists (most of us). With the exception of control charts, SPC tools are really just ways of organizing data. Their use and applications are rapidly expanding. Public

EXHIBIT 2–7
Statistical Process Control (SPC)

Process flow chart—A picture that describes the main steps, branches, and eventual outputs of a process.

Check sheet—An organized method for recording data.

Pareto analysis—A coordinated approach to identify rankings (e.g., of frequently made complaints); works to permanently eliminate defects. Focuses on important error sources. Applies the 80/20 rule: 80 percent of the problems are due to 20 percent of the causes.

Histogram—A distribution showing the frequency of occurrences between the high and low range of data.

Cause and effects diagram, or fishbone analysis—A tool that uses a graphical description of the process elements to analyze potential sources of process variation.

Run chart—A time sequence chart showing plotted values of a characteristic.

Scatter diagram—Also known as a *correlation chart.* A graph of the relationship of one characteristic to another characteristic.

Control chart—A time sequence chart showing plotted values of a statistic, including a central line and one or more statistically-derived control limits.

Source: Coopers and Lybrand, "Quality Practices" brochure, 1989.

utilities, for example, have in the past had little need or incentive to improve quality due to industry regulation and reduced competition. But things are changing. According to Mercer Management Consulting, more than one-half of electric and gas utilities are now using some form of TQM. Pacific Bell, for example, a San Francisco–based telephone company, has dropped its emphasis on cutting costs in favor of pursuing the broader challenge of quality service. *The Quality Primer: A Guide to Continuous Improvement* provides Pacific Bell's 60,000 employees with detailed instructions on basic quality techniques. The book has helped employees learn how to use basic techniques such as brainstorming, multivoting, flow charts, and histograms—all aimed ultimately at improving customer service and satisfaction.

But TQM, like other techniques borrowed from current Japanese practices, should be approached with some caution. Japanese management practices have proven troublesome for American businesses. Many U.S. firms have dropped their efforts to adopt Japanese techniques in favor of their own alternatives. Nevertheless, TQM is a control technique that can help maintain the quality of new processes and support efforts to raise quality levels in an organization.

CUSTOMER PREFERENCES

Speaking from their new San Francisco hotel adorned with four million dollars worth of art, antiques, Persian rugs, and English marble, Ritz-Carlton's president and chief operating officer, Horst Schulze, explained to his audience that accoutrements aren't everything. Drawing a comparison with banks, he said,

> You walk through the big entrance [in a bank], onto marble floors and through rows of marble pillars, and it all seems marvelous. There's a big counter of mahogany teller-windows. You are waiting to be called and suddenly you hear "Next!"
>
> You walk over to the teller who screamed at you but of course she is busy with her computer, so she doesn't look at you—at least not right away. Then, as she finally looks up at you—and there's absolutely no question about it—you know she hates you. You get in the car, and on the radio you hear that [same] bank advertising its quality service to customers. But ladies and gentlemen, tell me honestly, what do you remember: the marble pillar, the floor, the mahogany? Or the uncaring teller behind the counter?

The time, trouble, and expense of creating certain expectations can all be lost by not providing *what your customer considers important.*

For most products and services the importance of a particular attribute is often more important than its expected level. For example, the safety of an airline is considered more important than the quality of food it serves, no matter how delicious its meals are.

The quality of products and services contributes to customer satisfaction as do customer expectations. They are antecedents to customer satisfaction; but separately they have less of an effect on actual purchase than does overall consumer satisfaction.[17]

 A customer's perception of quality, however significant, is only part of his or her overall satisfaction with the product or service.

Simply measuring product quality from the customer's point of view won't ensure customer satisfaction. The attractiveness of a superbly crafted product will be outweighed by poor sales and service support, which irritates customers. Have you ever compromised quality by taking your business elsewhere because of poor service?

Although we may identify gaps between what customers expect and the quality they actually receive, we still need one more component before we can determine overall customer satisfaction. These gaps by themselves do not determine overall customer satisfaction. Remember, product quality, like customer expectations, is only part of what it takes to satisfy customers. We still need to account for individual customer preferences.

So far we have two of the three main ingredients that explain customer satisfaction. Expectations provide the foundation for customers to compare their experiences. This expectation-quality trade-off must be positive (i.e., the experience is at least as good as expected) if we are to satisfy customers at all. But to properly magnify this level of satisfaction, we must favor what customers prefer most. This is called *priority marketing* and is the final ingredient in the customer satisfaction formula.

Priority Marketing

Priority marketing focuses on what's important to the customer. What is important to one customer however, may not be as important to another. Consider the varying demands placed on an airport hotel: an airline stewardess may find 24-hour room service extremely valuable; a retired couple may need dietary menu options; a tour wholesaler may favor low prices; and a young female executive considers security a priority.

 Companies rarely break down products and services and ask customers what is important to them. This approach can yield very valuable insight about changing customer preferences.

It was once said that horses sweat, men perspire, and women glow. Procter and Gamble segmented the deodorant market by gender with Secret for women and Sure for men—alas, nothing for the poor horses. But two-way segmenting is not enough in today's competitive toiletry industry.

Grouping together customers who share similar priorities can offer an effective alternative to traditional customer segmentation. By identifying groups of customers who have similar preferences or even similar tastes (such as sharing common perceptions of quality or status), companies can target promotions to capitalize on known characteristics and individualize the presentation.

Discovering and taking advantage of consumer preferences is what priority marketing is all about. This approach is different from traditional market segmentation because it focuses on how customer priorities affect purchase decisions. It connects customers with products and services more effectively than traditional segmentation. Traditional segmentation focuses on customer demographics (age, sex, occupation, etc.) and does not relate the product or service to the customer. Specific attributes, such as age or gender, do not stimulate customers to spend money—individual preferences do. In this way, companies capitalize on knowing their customers. If Procter and Gamble learns that men who favor a menthol scent and aerosols in a black package with a picture of a bull on the label, then the company could promote these preferences in its advertising.

Companies use priority marketing in the same way when promoting services. Chemical Bank created a model that incorporates the relative importance of each service factor it measures. The firm then developed software based on the model to enable managers to manipulate service-measurement variables. Knowing these variables helps Chemical Bank decide where to allocate resources and it reveals service segments among its customers.

Priority marketing goes beyond traditional customer survey information by identifying information that can be closely related to actual product purchase. For example, if a customer rates your product as good or even excellent on a survey form, but never repurchases your product, you are likely to draw the wrong conclusion from the survey alone. Although it may be comforting to know that a customer likes your product, the reality is that this customer prefers a competitor's. It can be very misleading when no complaints are received or when surveys yield general observations about quality.

 *C*onsider *quality* separately from *importance*. Customer praise does not always equate to customer preference.[8]

Often, the reason companies don't provide what's important to customers is they simply don't know what customers prefer (Exhibit 2–8). For

EXHIBIT 2–8
Customers' Top Ten Service Characteristics

1. Employee attitude.
2. Receiving an explanation of how a problem happened.
3. Being called back when promised.
4. Being contacted promptly when a problem is resolved.
5. Being allowed to talk to someone in authority.
6. Being told how long it will take to solve a problem.
7. Being given useful alternatives if a problem can't be solved.
8. Providing sufficient information to act on alternatives.
9. Being told about ways to prevent a future problem.
10. Being given progress reports if a problem can't be solved immediately.

Source: Adapted from J. Barsky and S. Huxley, "A Customer-Survey Tool: Using the Quality Sample," *Cornell Hotel and Restaurant Administration Quarterly*, December 1992, p. 23; and Leonard L. Berry and A. Parasuraman, *Marketing Services*, (New York: Free Press, 1991), p. 39.

example, why is buying an automobile so complicated? We should be able to purchase a car as simply as we purchase a hamburger. X amount for the basic burger, Y for a double, and Z with extra cheese. There is no discussion, no ego battles, and no time wasted.

Employees or managers may think they're delivering what the customer wants, but inaccurate perceptions may be affecting their efforts. Persons often respond on the basis of their own priorities. What is most important to employees or managers may affect their perception of customer priorities.

 *E*mployees and management often have different views of what is important to the customer.

Have the effects of misreading customer preferences found their way into the activities of your firm? For example, employee performance standards and evaluations may not encourage what customers appreciate. Advertising and promotional materials may also emphasize things that aren't very important to target customers. The resources expended by an airline to improve its food may have more impact if the airline is also dedicated to keeping its flights on schedule.

 Products and services can be affected by misunderstanding customer preferences. Figure out how to redistribute resources to more accurately reflect customer priorities.

Measuring Preferences

After enjoying a great dinner at a friendly Italian restaurant, you might fill out a comment card as follows:

Expectations Met					Importance			
Not at All		Exceeded			Low		High	
1	②	3	4	FOOD	1	2	3	④
1	2	3	④	SERVICE	1	2	3	④
1	2	③	4	AMBIENCE	1	②	3	4

You selected the restaurant knowing they serve excellent food but were slightly disappointed—the eggplant was mushy and the meatballs tasteless. This was important because you're a fan of Italian cuisine. The disappointing food quality has affected your overall satisfaction and may affect your decision to return in the near future. If the manager of this restaurant was using a typical comment card, this dissatisfaction would go unnoticed.

 Service Wars
At a gathering of the world's leading bank executives at Tokyo's renowned Okura hotel, the topic of conversation during the coffee break was not finance. It was about the ability to open the hotel room door, toss the key onto a ledge, and have all the lights turn on. They all agreed that it was a great convenience to offer in an unfamiliar room and a sure way to prevent loss of keys.[9]

What does the term *importance* mean? Other words, such as *prominence*,[10] *intensity*,[11] and *active* versus *passive*,[12] have been used to describe the concept of importance. The concept of importance has even been equated with satisfaction itself.[13] Though not replacing satisfaction, the role of importance has been used in a variety of contexts in psychology[14] and marketing research.[15]

We shall utilize importance as the third and final component for determining customer satisfaction. The ratings of importance will reflect the relative value of various attributes to consumers. Lower ratings of importance are likely to play less of a role in affecting overall satisfaction. Higher importance ratings are likely to play a more critical role in determining customer satisfaction.

The purpose of measuring attribute importance is to identify which attributes, or combinations, are more responsible for purchase behavior and which have less impact. These attributes play a critical role in determining a customer's overall satisfaction with a product or service.

Putting the Pieces Together

We have reviewed all three components of customer satisfaction: expectations, quality, and importance. These will be combined into two separate variables to measure customer satisfaction:

1. *Expectations met*: Pre-experience beliefs about products or services compared to actual performance or perceptions of quality.

2. *Importance*: Customer priorities with respect to product or service components.

The next chapter examines the latest approaches to effectively communicating with customers and employees. Following this is an introduction to the Customer Satisfaction Scoring System (see page 65). This technique will combine customer input of these two variables into a customer satisfaction score. This approach has proven successful in industry[16] and is similar to the approach recently introduced by the Gallup Organization to rank the service quality of entire industries.

SUMMARY

Expectations

- Customers use the information provided about products and services to form expectations.
- The perception of superior performance can be eroded when preceded by exaggerated promises.
- Focus on improving areas where customer expectations are low and the value, or importance, to customers is high.
- Expectation levels should be set high enough to attract business but accurate enough to reflect the reality of what is likely to be delivered 100 percent of the time.
- Customer expectations will increase—so should your ability to meet and exceed them.
- Surprise is one way to exceed customer expectations. Promise what to expect, deliver this or more, and sometimes surprise customers.

Quality

- Americans are attracted to excellence and are willing to pay extra for quality.
- Management may estimate quality standards but customers have to refine them. These standards should include both production and use components.
- A customer's perception of quality, however significant, is only part of his or her overall satisfaction with the product or service.

Priority Marketing

- Companies rarely break down products and services and ask customers what is important to them. This approach can yield very valuable insight about changing customer preferences.
- Consider *quality* separately from *importance*. Customer praise does not always equate to customer preference.
- Employees and management often have different views of what is important to the customer.

- Products and services can be affected by misunderstanding customer preferences. Figure out how to redistribute resources to more accurately reflect customer priorities.

NOTES

1. Ernest R. Cadotte et al., "Expectations and Norms in Models of Consumer Satisfaction," *Journal of Marketing Research*, 24 (August 1987), pp. 305–14.

2. Leonard L. Berry and Linda R. Cooper, "Competing with Time-Saving Service" in *Managing Services* ed. Christopher H. Lovelock (Englewood Cliffs, NJ: Prentice Hall, 1993), p. 172.

3. From the "Vision Statement" for Residence Inn by Marriott.

4. Mary Rudie and J. Brant Wansley, "The Merrill Lynch Quality Program," Proceedings of American Marketing Association Services Marketing Conference, 1985, p. 9.

5. Ford no longer declares that quality is job one. The automaker is displacing *quality* with *consumer*. Refer to adjacent box.

6. Leonard L. Berry and A. Parasuraman, *Marketing Services* (New York: Free Press, 1991), p. 16.

7. Ibid.

8. Focusing on actual customer behavior instead of drawing conclusions based only on customer attitude or opinion (e.g., intention to buy product in future) is the heart of *outcomes measurement*, an emerging trend in management research.

9. From a speech by Richard Rosenburg, CEO, Bank of America, Hilton Hotel, San Francisco, March 15, 1993.

10. M. Fishbein and I. Ajzen, *Belief, Attitude, Intention, and Behavior* (Reading, MA: Addison Wesley, 1975), p. 221.

11. D. Katz, "The Functional Approach to the Study of Attitudes," *Public Opinion Quarterly* 24 (1960), pp. 163–204.

12. "Attitudes, even when indistinguishable from each other as measured by a questionnaire or survey, can have either an active or passive character." Dennis W. Organ and Thomas S. Bateman, *Organizational Behavior* (Homewood, IL: Irwin, 1991), p. 162.

13. M. J. Rosenberg, "Cognitive Structure and Attitudinal Affect," *Journal of Abnormal and Social Psychology* 53 (1956), pp. 356–72.

14. See, for example, N. H. Anderson, "Functional Measurement and Psycho-Physical Judgement," *Psychological Review* 77 (1970), pp. 153–70.

15. For example, attribute importance has been studied as a component in determining job satisfaction. Patricia Smith Mikes and Charles L. Hulin, "Use of Importance as a Weighing Component of Job Satisfaction," *Journal of Applied Psychology* 52 (1968): pp. 394–98.

16. Jonathan D. Barsky and Richard Labagh, "A Strategy for Customer Satisfaction," *Cornell Hotel and Restaurant Administration Quarterly*, October 1992, p. 31–42.

17. J. J. Cronin, Jr., and Steven Taylor, "Measuring Service Quality: A Reexamination and Extension" *Journal of Marketing*, July 1992, p. 55–68.

Chapter Three

Listening to Customers and Employees

Engaging Customers and Employees in Feedback and Problem-Solving Activities

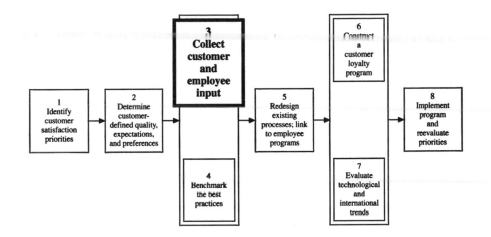

They just go along their merry way, providing the products or services that they think *their customers want, and then work like hell to convince their customers this is what they need.*

H. Brad Antin and Alan J. Antin, *Secrets From the Lost Art of Common Sense Marketing*

Understanding the perceptions of the customer is crucial to service success.

Karl Albrecht and Ron Zemke, *Service America*

47

Garfield is gone. That cute cartoon-cat, borrowed in 1984 to introduce Embassy Suites, Inc., is no longer useful to the 25th largest hotel company.[1] Embassy Suites' business travelers (two-thirds of their clientele) don't care about cuteness in a hotel; they want a clean, spacious room, friendly service, and complete facilities—at a good price. Hence, their new ad theme, "Why choose any hotel when you can get *twice the hotel* . . . at Embassy Suites."

Embassy Suites based this decision on the results of a variety of customer feedback techniques: traditional comment cards; face-to-face minisurveys; a 100 percent guarantee program, in which failures served as a constant and precise evaluation tool; and a mail survey. The mail survey, called the Guest Satisfaction Rating System, is Embassy Suites' principal source of guest information. The company sends this 48-point questionnaire with $1 to its recent guests. About 50,000 guests per year return the questionnaires, a 50 percent response rate.

An increasing number of companies are using such a combined approach for gathering feedback. For example, Marriott uses "mystery guests" and discussions with guests in addition to their traditional comment card system called the Guest Service Index (GSI) program. Their Residence Inn properties (for travelers staying five or more nights) survey both current guests (guest tracking) and potential guests (market tracking).

 World-class companies use a combination of customer feedback methods, both common (surveys, complaint/suggestion cards, 800 numbers, focus groups) and uncommon (mystery shoppers, spotters, computer-aided questionnaires).

POWER LISTENING: YOU CAN'T AFFORD NOT TO LISTEN

Listening to the customer is essential. Following customer directions helped make Saturn, introduced in 1990, one of the U.S. auto industry's most successful product launches ever. During its first two years, the General Motors subsidiary sold more cars per dealer than any other brand.

---

[1] *1991 Directory of Hotel & Motel Systems* American Hotel and Motel Association.

Of course, every company would like to believe that it listens to its customers as well as Embassy Suites or Saturn. Unfortunately, customers don't speak clearly or in unison. Most companies just assume they know what their customers want. But assumptions can be very dangerous.

Research has shown that although we spend most of our time at work listening (9 percent writing, 16 percent reading, 25 percent talking, and 50 percent listening), most of us don't listen very well. We retain, on average, only 25 percent of what we hear. This listening gap is magnified when it affects communication with our customers. If employees retain only 25 percent of all the complaints, suggestions, and compliments heard from customers in a day, imagine how much crucial information is lost.

Big companies sometimes substitute complicated research for real interaction with customers. But any company can listen with little added expense. Tom Peters, in his book *Thriving on Chaos*, advises companies to become obsessed with listening. "the race will go to those who listen most intently (and respond)."[2]

Although there are success stories of companies that didn't rely on customer input to develop new opportunities (e.g., Wal-Mart's choosing to locate near small to mid-size markets) their intuition correctly anticipated consumer response. Perhaps it was luck. Efforts to obtain financing, or simply to gain the support of others, benefit from some evidence of customer support.

World-class companies do not become overconfident and complacent with success. Companies such as Ritz-Carlton, Rolls-Royce, Motorola, and L.L. Bean make sure they understand the changing needs of their clientele and use this information for improving products and services, employee training, and other customer retention strategies. They work hard to avoid the common pitfalls experienced by some mature organizations: sliding standards, indifference to customers, and the belief that they can do no wrong. World-class companies avoid this downward spiral by staying in touch with customers. The communication process begins with getting customers involved well before a product or service is delivered to the public.

Get Customers Involved Early

In creating the successful AS/400, IBM involved customers, field personnel, and business partners throughout the planning and development stages. They invited a group of customers to Rochester, New York, where the hardware and software plans were being developed. This customer advisory council discussed their suggestions and reactions to these plans

with IBM's management and staff. The company involved other customers in an early availability program by putting the product in working customer environments. Field personnel communicated with customers and
suppliers to detect unforeseen issues that needed attention. IBM also provided software to business partners so they would be knowledgeable when
the hardware was available.

IBM, Rochester, is the exception. Companies still fail to involve the customer sufficiently. Historic blunders, such as Ford Motor Company's Edsel
losing approximately $250 million, demonstrate that rushing to market has
taken precedence over patiently conferring with customers. GM released
the Cadillac Allante before many customer-detected errors were resolved.
PepsiCo nearly matched Coca-Cola's infamous blunder of the sweeter New
Coke with Pepsi A.M., a new version of Pepsi for breakfast. Anheuser-
Busch and Coors failed to heed the cries of customers who didn't understand what dry beer was. Even seasoned beer drinkers couldn't figure out
the new product's unique benefits—was it the opposite of wet beer?[3]

The top priority of a new program involving the combined forces of
Procter & Gamble Co., Apple Computer Inc., Hewlett-Packard, Motorola, Colgate Palmolive, and Chrysler is to figure out how invention, in-
house teamwork, and customer involvement can improve their products
and services. Companies can double their profits by improving the success rate of product and service introductions.[4]

 World-class customer satisfaction requires frequent communication with customers, employees, and competitors. The
process begins with getting customers involved well before a
product or service is delivered to the public.

We will focus on how organizations can stay in touch with customer
perceptions of current products and services.

Surveys

Hewlett-Packard spends nearly $1 million annually on surveys for its ser-
vice support, a $2 billion business, and invests heavily in surveying its
competition and customers. They also conduct informal interviews, focus
groups, and small scale surveys.

La Quinta Motor Inns attributes much of its recent success to a variety
of guest feedback programs:[5]

EXHIBIT 3–1
Customer Feedback Methods

Surveys

Comment cards

Mail, phone, in-person, and computer questionnaires

Other approaches

Suggestion boxes

800 telephone numbers

Focus groups

Customer advisory councils

Employee feedback

Management observation and interaction with customers

Spotters

Role playing (confederates or mystery customers)

Customer visits

Sales data and other research

- *Monthly guest surveys.* Each month, 400 guests are selected at random and asked to complete a questionnaire. A dollar incentive is included in the mailing. The response rate is approximately 40 percent compared to an average of 1 to 5 percent that would reply without the dollar incentive.
- *Monthly club surveys.* Each month, 400 members of the Returns Club, La Quinta's frequent travelers club, are sent a questionnaire similar to that used in the monthly guest survey but with added focus on club services (types of perks preferred and so forth). The response rate is slightly higher with these guests, 42 percent.
- *In-room comment cards.* These are placed in each guest room.
- *Toll-free guest assistance center (GAC).* The 800 telephone number appears in the annual directory of La Quinta Hotels. The type of inquiries are tracked and used as a form of guest feedback.

Like Hewlett-Packard and La Quinta, most world-class companies use a combination of methods to maintain a dialogue with customers. Exhibit 3–1 presents various feedback methods.

No single feedback method is best for all situations. The objective of your project and time and cost constraints determine which approach is best. Exhibit 3–2 provides a grading system to use when deciding on survey methods.

EXHIBIT 3–2
Grading Survey Methods

Constraints	Comment Card	Mail Survey	Telephone Interview	Personal Interview	Computer Survey	Focus Group
Level of detail*	C	D	B	A	B	A
Time	B	D	A	B	B-	B
Money	A	B	B-	C	C	A-

A = excellent, B = good, C = fair, D = poor.

*Level of detail = Will your survey require detailed information (over 15 questions or qualitative information)?

Although the approach to each method may differ, well-designed surveys share certain characteristics. To be most useful, surveys should:

- Ask what customers think of current offerings.
- Solicit comments and suggestions for improvements.
- Collect demographic information and data on buying behavior.
- Use a format that identifies *expectations met* and the *importance* of products or services.
- Offer sufficient incentives to improve the response rate and enhance the accuracy of findings.
- Be distributed in a systematic, random fashion (e.g., every third customer; each customer wearing blue; the fifth person appearing on each page of a customer list).
- Be analyzed along with other forms of customer feedback.

It's simple—if you want to know what customers want, ask them. You can measure how satisfied customers are with your product, service, company, and personnel by considering how well their expectations are being met and what is important to them. Exhibit 3–3 presents a sample customer survey used to generate feedback from hotel guests.

Problems with Surveys

On July 6, 1992, the media announced that "Perot leads Bush 36 percent to 31 percent" (Times Mirror Co. survey), "Bush leads Perot 32 percent to 30 percent" (*New York Times*/CBS Poll), and "Perot leads Bush 36 percent to 30 percent" (ABC News survey).

EXHIBIT 3–3
Sample Guest Satisfaction Survey

Thank you for staying with us! Please help us provide better service to you by answering this short questionnaire.

Expectations Met					Importance			
Not at all		Exceeded			Low			High
1	2	3	4	Location	1	2	3	4
1	2	3	4	Parking	1	2	3	4
1	2	3	4	Check-in/out	1	2	3	4
				Room				
1	2	3	4	Cleanliness	1	2	3	4
1	2	3	4	Comfort	1	2	3	4
				Services provided				
1	2	3	4	Business	1	2	3	4
1	2	3	4	Leisure	1	2	3	4
				Employee attitudes				
1	2	3	4	Reception	1	2	3	4
1	2	3	4	Restaurants	1	2	3	4
				Hotel facilities				
1	2	3	4	Appearance	1	2	3	4
1	2	3	4	Condition	1	2	3	4
				Overall				
1	2	3	4	Atmosphere	1	2	3	4
1	2	3	4	Price/value	1	2	3	4

How likely is it that you will return to this hotel?

Not likely   1   2   3   4   Very likely

Purpose of your visit: ___ business ___ pleasure

Are you with: ___ a tour   ___ individual

___ a meeting/convention   ___ an airline

Have you stayed at this hotel before? ___ Yes ___ No

Did you consider other hotels for this trip?
___ Yes ___ No   If yes, which one(s)? _____

_____

Why did you consider these other hotel(s)? _____

Why did you select *this* hotel? _____

Please give us any other comments you feel would help us (use back if necessary):

_____

PLEASE TURN IN AT THE FRONT DESK.
THANK YOU VERY MUCH!

As it turned out, no one really had any idea who was ahead—Clinton, the eventual winner, finished third in these polls. Ever since it was predicted that Dewey would defeat Truman, polls have not been taken too seriously. The problem is that as more organizations contact us at home and work and on the street, less of us are willing to participate in these surveys, or polls. The mixed and often conflicting results shown by these polls are therefore dangerously misleading.

A major problem of surveys is the refusal rate—when a large portion, about 36 percent for political polls, of the sample population refuses to respond. Worse, those who don't respond tend to be the "trendsetters," the younger, more affluent customers who are likely to influence others in politics and consumer trends.

Customers walk away from mall pollsters, hang up on telemarketers, and throw away mail surveys because they think the researchers are really trying to sell them something.

Surveys for consumer products and services have even higher refusal rates than political polls. Typically, these short questionnaires or comment cards are placed in guest rooms, restaurants, cocktail lounges, airline seat pockets, and so forth. They are also often available from cashiers or hostesses. Any customer may elect to participate in these surveys, but most don't.

Who fills out customer comment cards? Is it the vacationer who has more time? Are women more inclined to express their opinion? Are first-time visitors more interested in filling out these forms? Whatever the motive for participating, these casual surveys are of dubious value in terms of accurately representing customers. Persons who participate in these surveys are self-selected and are not representative of those who don't participate. Randomly selected participants would more accurately reflect the true population.[6] Survey refusal represents an everyday example of what marketers fear most: consumer apathy.

There is also a tendency for companies to write self-serving questionnaires. Chrysler found that test drivers preferred Chryslers to Toyotas; the paper bag industry found that shoppers preferred paper bags.

Let's look at the common problems experienced with surveys and how to solve them.

Worthless or misleading information. Traditional customer surveys provide little or inaccurate information to support informed decision making. Consider the following example.

John B. Corporate, staying at the Bed 'n Business Hotel is concerned about location, price, and a comfortable bed. He completed only the first two questions on a guest comment card:

1. Was check-in courteous and efficient?
   Excellent _X_ Good__ Fair__ Poor__
2. Bell staff: Were they helpful, informative, and prompt?
   Excellent _X_ Good__ Fair__ Poor__

How helpful is this information? John never came back to this hotel. Poorly constructed guest surveys don't measure what they are intended to. The solution is to improve the guest survey by asking the right questions.

1. Questions should focus on the customer-important attributes of products and services. Place them in the order that reflects a typical customer's experience—similar to the customer cycle. Make sure to include questions covering the full range of products and services that are important to customers.

2. Questions relating to service can address such issues as accuracy (Was your car repaired correctly?); completeness (Was anything left undone?); timeliness of service (Was it completed on time?); and behavior and attitude of employees (Was the staff courteous?).

3. For each attribute, survey questions should measure what *causes* satisfaction. How well did we meet your expectations? How important are these services to you? Referring to our example above, John B. Corporate responds with:

Expectations Met					Importance			
Not at all		*Exceeded*			*Low*			*High*
1	2	③	4	Check-in	1	2	③	4
1	2	③	4	Bell Staff	1	2	③	4
1	2	③	4	Price (value)	1	2	③	4
①	2	3	4	Parking	1	2	3	④

How likely is it that you will return to this hotel?

Not likely ① 2 3 4 Very likely

This guest is *not* coming back. The source of dissatisfaction appears in this survey approach. Note the response to parking ($19 per night): a very low expectations met score with a high importance rating.

4. In addition to the product and service questions, is anything else important to the customer? Do they have any ideas for improvements or suggestions, comments? Leave plenty of space. Ask for demographic information (age, income) and about buying behavior (When do you purchase? How often? How do you especially enjoy using our product or service?).

5. Other valuable questions may be developed to answer the following:

   • What do customers want out of this product or service?
   • What or how are we missing?
   • How can we better provide what customers want?
   • What competing brands have they purchased?
   • How are these competitors superior?
   • What else could be added to improve the customer experience?
   • How much more are they willing to pay? For what additional products/services?
   • Who are the customers and how can they be reached? Ask for name (optional), address, and phone number.
   • What is the customer's occupation, life stage, and so forth.

6. Make the survey introduction and closing both friendly and professional (as shown in Exhibit 3–4). Thank them for their efforts.

7. Try to keep most questions close ended (structured) with specific answers to choose from (numbers or multiple choice). Limit fill-in-the-blank answers to numbers or other factual information (e.g., list of competitive brands used).

Customer apathy.   Another common problem with surveys is that, typically, only the most happy or unhappy customers fill them out. Often, certain customer segments (for example, corporate and other frequent hotel guests tend not to participate in surveys. Japanese customers prefer not to fill out comment cards at all. A poor-quality sample—typically the result of a self-selection process—generates unreliable information and leads to errors. Some businesses will even try to boost their customer satisfaction ratings by asking buyers to fill out rating forms in the presence of a salesperson or manager. Under a watchful eye customers feel intimidated and modify their responses to avoid confrontation.

However, response rates of surveys need not be low and unrepresentative of some customer segments. By focusing on the following areas, a company can conduct a quality survey that provides reliable information regarding all customer segments.

Convenience

- Place surveys in customers' path and where they may have an extra moment to concentrate. Examples include at cash registers or sent with regular billing statements, directly to customer. Go beyond familiar locations. Leaving surveys in unusual places will help to call attention to them.
- Ask simple and precise questions; avoid hard-to-answer questions like "Were you satisfied?" or "Was this a quality experience?" Focus questions on aspects of product and service use.
- Keep it short, from 10 to 15 questions.
- Make drop off or collection easy. For example, in a hotel, avoid mail returns for comment cards distributed in-house.

Incentives (tangible)[7]

- Incentives are effective means to encourage survey participation. But they must provide sufficient reward to motivate.
- Quality of incentive must be consistent with firm's image; for example, not a cheap gift for a first-class business.
- Receipt of the incentive or gift must be hassle-free.

Encouragement (intangible)

- Make a personal request to complete survey.
- Use additional promotion, words of encouragement, show of appreciation, and so forth.
- Ask interesting or fun questions. Present questions and answers professionally.
- Give customers the feeling that their answers will not be tampered with. Make it clear that survey will be reviewed by a person of authority and kept confidential.
- Subsequent contacts are often sufficient to prompt a response. A postcard or brief phone call a short time following purchase can be very effective.

A recent hotel study[8] accomplished a nearly 100 percent response rate by using the following specific techniques:

- Personal distribution at check-in.
- Special request letter from the general manager (Exhibit 3–4).
- High-quality presentation.
- Gift incentive—choice of a bottle of fine California wine, a box of See's chocolates, or a $10 discount off the customer's bill.
- Verbal encouragement at checkout.

Consumer apathy is a problem with most surveys. Nonetheless, many researchers consider 15 to 20 percent a usable response rate even when this results in a small sample size.[9] Despite substantial research on improving survey response rates[10] (including modifications in questionnaire design, alternative distribution methods, and incentives for responding), there is no strong evidence supporting the effectiveness of any technique other than the use of monetary incentives[11] or making follow-up contacts.

 *G*et more customer feedback by focusing on the convenience aspects of survey execution and by offering incentives to stimulate customer participation.

Some successful mail-order companies, such as Land's End, L.L. Bean, and Children's Wear Digest, use comment cards. Most insert the cards (with return postage) in every shipment or catalog sent. Although only 10 to 15 percent respond, these companies consider the information from these cards in decision making. For example, L.L. Bean found that direct mail customers are especially sensitive to delivery time. This led to creating better forecasting and inventory methods. Fulfillment processes were restructured for efficiency and to allow for special and rush orders. Quick responses allow customers to make additional orders during the same fashion season.

Innovative approaches to making customer input more convenient can improve response rates. Panasonic attaches reply cards to each product sold. Dell Computer includes a questionnaire diskette when it delivers computers. IKEA furniture conducts in-store surveys. Volkswagen, Europe's automobile market leader, uses a widespread distribution approach to survey about 660,000 customers in Germany every two years.

EXHIBIT 3–4
Special Request Letter to Encourage Survey Response

This cover letter was attached to the customer survey using the quality sample approach.

Dear Guest (use customer name if possible):

Welcome to the _____ Hotel!
You have been selected to participate in an important guest service study. As one of a very small group, your participation is crucial to the success of this study. In return for your efforts, you may select from several nice gifts:

- A bottle of fine California wine
- A box of Godiva Chocolates
- $10 discount off your bill

Please complete the attached form, bring it with you to the front desk at check-out (or towards the end of your stay) and pick up a gift in appreciation for your efforts.
Your thoughtful response is very important to us and will receive my personal attention.
Thank you for staying with us.

Sincerely,

General Manager

Other approaches to soliciting more customer comments include Fidelity Bank's "service labs" where customers are asked, in exchange for lunch, to test prototypes of forms, pamphlets, and other services. These meetings have resulted in simplifying the bank's automated telephone prompts, recording softer-voiced instructions, and expanding their number of toll-free numbers.

Some European companies also realize the value of improved response rates. Bang & Olufsen, the Danish consumer electronics manufacturer, extends their guarantee for another year for customers who respond to a questionnaire. Dell Computer thanks the respondents with 10 free diskettes.

World-class organizations have mechanisms that make it easy for customers to comment on product or service quality. They actively follow up with customers to encourage feedback and to build their client relationships. The challenge is to develop and maintain a combination of approaches to systematically obtain customer input and reactions (e.g., surveys, interviews, focus groups, and so on).

Despite the shortcomings of surveys caused by nonresponse bias (refusal rate), poor design, and limited market research, managers tend to put much stock in the information provided by surveys.[12] The end result can be poor decision making. Decisions based on such surveys will yield only partial information and may be dangerously misleading. Management should also consider other approaches to obtain customer information and improve their current survey method (refer to Exhibit 3–1).

Focus Groups

Focus groups have been used much more in the last 10 years by a wide variety of industries. These groups are used as a tool for improving customer service and for developing and testing products and services. Details for implementing your own focus groups are provided in Step 3 in Chapter 8.

Service Wars
Cable network Nickelodeon set up a consumer focus group on a computer network to get new ideas and spontaneous feedback on shows from 75 children from across the United States.

Typically, a focus group is composed of customers, typically about 6 to 12, from each of the organization's major market segments. A separate focus group may also be conducted for internal customers (employees). A moderator either presents an issue for discussion or participants will initiate their own concerns.

A sample format for a customer focus group is as follows. Participants first review their actual product or service experience. A moderator then asks them what their ideal product or service experience would be like. The participants select a top five list in order of priority. The session ends with a discussion of how products or services could resemble their ideal scenario.

Following the session, the moderator or manager writes down the results of the session. The customer suggestions may be used as the subject for an internal customer focus group.

In an internal customer focus group, four to seven employees partake in an informal discussion with management. The results of the customer focus group are distributed. A moderator asks the other employees to comment on customers' ideas. The discussion focuses on implementation of improvements for each customer segment.

The customer focus group is valuable for prompting feedback from a cross-section of customers about problems they have experienced and their solutions and ideal scenarios. The employee focus group can explore how these customer suggestions may be implemented and enhanced. Customer and employee input is critical to improve the design and delivery of customer processes (Chapter 5).

Telemarketing

Telephone interviewing gathers information quickly and provides greater flexibility than mail questionnaires. Telemarketing has increased dramatically as a result of improvements in technology, a lack of legal restrictions, and better consumer lists.

The Washington based TARP Institute (Technical Research Assistance Program) and Alland Research, for example, rely on computerized telephone systems to reach consumers. These companies conduct customer satisfaction surveys for the public as well as for companies such as Coca-Cola, American Express, General Motors, Chrysler, Mitsubishi, and 600 auto dealers nationwide. Their network of computerized telephone systems reach consumers usually within 10 days after a major purchase (over $150). This information, supplemented by questionnaires sent to consumers' homes, is stored in computer databanks. Complaints are relayed quickly to the client, merchant, or manufacturer. All of the data is evaluated for how clients can strengthen their customers' satisfaction and how loyalty can be improved.

The popularity of computer-assisted telephone interviewing and other random calling approaches has, however, created a credibility problem. Many people resist automated dialing efforts or other cold call approaches. These approaches have a long way to go before they will seem truly personal. Computer calls that feel less impersonal and become more efficient in servicing customers will offer the best results (See Chapter 7).

800 Telephone Numbers

Most 800 numbers support the order-taking process. They are easily remembered ("Call 1-800-DENTIST") and are free to the calling party. (Do you remember this number: 800-325-3535? It's a well-known telephone number around the world: Sheraton Hotels' International Reservation hot line.) They can also play a big role. General Electric's G.E. Answer Center receives over three million calls per year, about 30 percent of which come from customers inquiring about products and services. For these customers, the free phone service provides a broader marketing function by providing information. For General Electric, increased product knowledge and more time committed to purchase decisions led to increased sales.

Toll-free phone service is an inexpensive method of encouraging and facilitating customer contact. This customer service gives the impression of professionalism and quality even though start-up costs and maintenance fees are cheap. Significant costs are incurred only if many long distance calls are received. However, these usually more than pay for themselves with increased sales and greater market exposure.

Computer Surveys

Based on a scale of 0 to 10, with 10 being the highest, computers are scoring 8s and above. Interviewers carry pen-based computers on their arms, question customers, and check off answers on the screen. Within hours after talking with the last customer, the interviewer can process and analyze the data. Even statistical measures that used to require a trained statistician can be applied almost instantly. Recent highlights of computer based surveys include:

- Mervyn's switched their advertising to a country and western radio station when a last minute survey of Christmas shoppers revealed this preference.
- Campbell and Kraft present customers with words, pictures, and videos using IdeaMap (Moskowitz, Jacobs Inc., Valhalla, New York). Their reactions are used as early input into the design of products.
- An interesting application developed by Populus Inc. (Boise, Idaho) has the computer calculate while it's interviewing. It designs each successive question based on the previous answer. This is the same

principle that the emerging technologies of artificial intelligence and expert systems are based on (see Chapter 7).

Advocates claim people are willing to divulge more private information during computer interviewing. If, for example, you ask someone, face to face, what their income is, they're likely to say "none of your business". On the computer, it's an anonymous transaction.

One popular method is to send questionnaires on disks. Response rates are improved for persons who prefer computers over pencil and paper; in addition, people can't tell how long the questionnaire will be. Another method, called *feedback clipboard*, uses a special electronic box with a small screen and 12 buttons. Developed by Feedback Marketing Services Corporation of Wellesley, Massachusetts, it resembles a telephone and gets extremely quick results. In-house computer surveys are also possible. With this method, questions appear on the screen and respondents answer via a console. This approach is fast, offers flexibility to change questions, and reduces interviewer bias.

Marriott's Fairfield Inn uses this in-house approach in a game format called *Scorecard*. Based on a simple PC-driven survey, this checkout game requires only about 15 seconds to play. An automated comment card encourages guests to provide feedback on the cleanliness of their room, the level of hospitality at check-in and check-out, and the overall value of their experience. In contrast to Marriott's more traditional room questionnaire, which yields a 5 percent response rate, this automated game card yields an average 50 percent response rate and provides more information. Guest responses are keyed to the times they were filled out and provide daily customer feedback by employee.

Spotters and Mystery Shoppers

Spotters are persons who spy on an operation to monitor, measure, and evaluate performance. Mystery shoppers, on the other hand, actually pretend to be customers and base their assessment on their direct experiences. Sometimes these two approaches are combined. Some airlines, for instance, hire people to fly various routes and assess every aspect of their operation, from ticketing to luggage handling to in-flight service and comfort.

Customer Visits

In many cases managers, engineers, and other employees can obtain useful information by visiting customers at their place of business. This makes perfect sense if your product or service is consumed at your customers' place of business because you can see it in action. But even if your customers don't use your product or service at their place of business, you can gain insight into hidden customer characteristics or preferences (what the customer feels comfortable with) through observation and discussions. Key considerations for customer visits include knowing what the objective of each visit is; preparing a discussion guide; knowing how many visits to make and to how many different customers; and analyzing data carefully without overgeneralizing. The primary advantages of visiting customers are that it shows your concern and it collects immediate feedback.[13]

Simple Surveys

Customer research does not need to be conducted by experts or in large companies with big budgets. Evaluations need not be formal. Managers with little time or money, such as those in small businesses, can use many of the techniques described in this chapter using less formal or scaled-down approaches. For example, managers can be given tapes of customer feedback recorded on your company's toll-free customer hot line to listen to in their cars. This helps to keep employees sensitive to the concerns of customers and will likely generate a range of solutions to customer problems.

Observation is a useful technique for assessing customers. Managers can identify their customer mix by recording how many and what kinds of customers shop in their stores at different times. Competitor advertising can also be monitored by simply collecting ads from the local media.

Surveys can be conducted using small samples. Inviting small groups of customers to lunch can provide many of the advantages of a more formal focus group. Talking to customers in the store, random phone calls to customers, and talking candidly with employees can provide valuable information.

One unusual approach to assessing customer satisfaction is used by Sun Microsystems. Executives take turns in a "listening booth" at trade shows to experience customer reaction. And much like car companies

EXHIBIT 3–5
Informal Customer Feedback

Casual observation

Customer mix and behavior
Competitors' customers; promotions, and so forth.

Casual discussions

Customer phone calls, talks, lunches, and so forth.
Employee comments
Supplier comments

Simple surveys

Small convenience samples.

have started doing, they call customers within the first several months for their reactions and add this to their database to track changes in buyers' needs and perceptions. Informal feedback approaches are listed in Exhibit 3–5.

Service Wars
The Swedish government now uses customer satisfaction data to assess its country's productivity. Sweden is the first country to develop and maintain an index dedicated exclusively to customer satisfaction. This new index measures the quality of products and services as experienced by the buyer and will be used to affect general economic policy for the entire country.

THE CUSTOMER SATISFACTION SCORING SYSTEM

The biggest advantage gained by surveying customers is the ability to focus on what needs improvement. If we know how products and services affect customers today, we can focus on improving products and services to provide greater satisfaction in the future. The challenge is to use the survey results to make changes that anticipate the increasing expectations of these customers. If these same customers return, they should not be disappointed.

 *I*f we know how products and services affect customers today, we can focus on providing greater satisfaction in the future.

Customer satisfaction is created by exceeding expectations, delivering quality, and targeting customer preferences (Chapter 2). The questionnaire presented in Exhibit 3–3 includes these three dimensions. The expectations met question inquires about both the expectation and quality aspects of a customer experience, while the importance question reveals customer preferences. The answers to these questions are combined to form the customer satisfaction score. In other words, the responses on the expectations met side of the survey are combined with the corresponding importance responses on the right side of the survey. However, due to the nature of this relationship, a special approach is necessary to represent the data generated by both these aspects of the survey. Consider the following example:

Guest A was a foreign traveler who was staying for a short time. Although he spent most of his time experiencing the city's finest restaurants and entertainment, he did have one light breakfast in his room. Guest B, on the other hand, was a business traveler who was busy meeting with clients all day. So, when he returned to the hotel very late each evening, he depended on room service for dinner. Although dissatisfied, he continued using room service for each of his five nights at the hotel. Unfortunately for Guest B, the room service at this hotel had been experiencing some real problems in food quality as a result of staff turnover. One question from each of the two guests' comment cards revealed the following:

	Expectations Met					*Importance*			
	Not at All		*Exceeded*			*Low*			*High*
Guest A:	1	2	3	④	Room service	①	2	3	4
Guest B:	①	2	3	4	Room service	1	2	3	④

Simply multiplying the number on the left (expectations met) with the number on the right (importance) would provide equal scores of 4. Surely, these customers were not satisfied equally as these numbers would indicate. To calculate customer satisfaction scores that accurately reflect the data, the following customer satisfaction scoring matrix was developed:

			Importance			
			Low 1	2	3	High 4
	Not at All	1	-1.5	-3.0	-4.5	-6.0
Expectations Met		2	-.5	-1.0	-1.5	-2.0
		3	.5	1.0	1.5	2.0
	Exceeded	4	1.5	3.0	4.5	6.0

Using this new scale, expectations met may now be combined with importance. The customer satisfaction score for Guest A is now 1.5 and for Guest B is -6. These scores are a better indicator of the actual guest experiences. The lowest customer satisfaction score is -6 (worst) and the highest is 6 (best). The objective of your project should focus on one of the lowest customer satisfaction scores. Give special preference to the area that has the biggest potential for improving customer satisfaction. This is an area with a low expectations met score and a high importance score. See the Preliminary Step in Chapter 8 to adapt this scoring system to your needs.

 Computer programs are a big help in processing and analyzing all types of surveys. Several software programs are very simple to use.

Whether customer feedback is obtained by phone, mail, questionnaire, or in-person survey, the key is to analyze the information promptly, to identify and resolve problems (or prevent them from occurring), and to discover opportunities as they develop. Numerous computer programs are available to help with this process, as listed in Exhibit 3–6.

EXHIBIT 3–6
Computer Software for Customer Surveys

- *Survey Pro.* This survey-producing program also performs basic analysis: tables, graphs, percents, means, open-ended answers and cross-tabulations. Exportable database. Apian Software, PO Box 1224, Menlo Park, CA 94026; (800) 237-4565.
- *ABSURV & WINSTAR.** These integrate with windows. They are for serious survey analysis but are easy to use given their capabilities. Excellent program for beginner or advanced. Anderson-Bell Corp., PO Box 5160 Arvada, CO 80005; (303) 940-0595.
- *Customer Support Activity Manager.* This tracks 800-number inquiries, how quickly customer service reps resolve problems, what type of calls are coming in, and so forth. Richard Brock, Brock Control Systems; Atlanta, GA; (404) 431-1200.
- *Object Vision for Windows.* Excellent new program creates surveys and visual business applications: spreadsheets, database management, forms—everything but word processing. Inquire about their video. Borland, 100 Borland Way, Scotts Valley, CA 95067; (800) 331-0877 or (408) 438-8400.
- *Surveyor.* A PC-based program lets you compose questionnaires, enter data, and analyze in variety of ways, including true cross-tabulations and other statistics. CFMC, 547 Howard Street, San Francisco, CA 94105; (415) 777-0470.

*Author's preference.

SUMMARY

- World-class companies use a combination of customer feedback methods, both common (surveys, complaint/suggestion cards, 800 numbers, focus groups) and uncommon (mystery shopper, spotters, computer-aided questionnaires).
- World-class customer satisfaction requires frequent communication with customers, employees, and competitors. The process begins with getting customers involved well before a product or service is delivered to the public.
- Get more customer feedback by focusing on the convenience aspects of survey execution and by offering incentives and other encouragements to stimulate customer participation.
- If we know how products and services affect customers today, we can focus on providing greater satisfaction in the future.
- Computer programs are a big help in processing and analyzing all types of surveys. Several software programs are very simple to use.

NOTES

1. *1991 Directory of Hotel & Motel Systems,* American Hotel and Motel Association.
2. Tom Peters, *Thriving on Chaos* (New York: Alfred A. Knopf, 1987).
3. "Flops," *Business Week,* August 16, 1993, p. 77.
4. According to Yoram Wind, professor of marketing, at University of Pennsylvania's Wharton School of Business.
5. This section is based on information provided by John Kaegi, vice president of marketing, and Isaac Jon Collazo, marketing information manager, from La Quinta's corporate headquarters, San Antonio, Texas.
6. A major issue in determining quality levels in manufacturing is when a sample doesn't contain any defects. How many defects should then be reported? The assumption is that (1) defects do exist, and (2) even a random sample cannot provide complete information. This underscores the importance of conducting a high-quality random sample.
7. For additional information, see Betsy S. Gelb, "Incentives to Increase Survey Returns: Social Class Considerations," *Journal of Marketing Research* 12 (February 1975), p. 107.
8. Jonathan D. Barsky and Stephen J. Huxley, "The Quality Sample," *The Cornell University Hotel and Restaurant Administration Quarterly,* December 1992, pp. 18–25.
9. Julie Yu and Harris Cooper, "A Quantitative Review of Research Design Effects on Response Rates to Questionnaires," *Journal of Marketing Research* 20 (February 1983), p. 36.
10. Stephen J. Huxley, "Predicting Response Speed in Mail Surveys," *Journal of Marketing Research* 17 (February 1980), pp. 63–68; Scott J. Armstrong, "Monetary Incentives in Mail Surveys," *Public Opinion Quarterly* 39 (1975), pp. 111–16; and Leslie Kanuk and Conrad Bereson, "Mail Surveys and Response Rates: A Literature Review, *Journal of Marketing Research* 12 (November 1975), pp. 440–53.
11. Monetary incentives may be either given up front (unconditional) or only after questionnaire return (conditional). See, for example, Gelb, "Incentives to Increase Survey Returns," p. 107.
12. Ashton D. Trice and H. Layman, "Improving Guest Surveys," *The Cornell University Hotel and Restaurant Administration Quarterly,* November 1984, p. 10.
13. Edward F. McQuarrie, *Customer Visits* (Beverly Hills, CA: Sage Publishers, 1993).

Chapter Four

Benchmarking for Competitive Advantage
Overtaking Your Competition

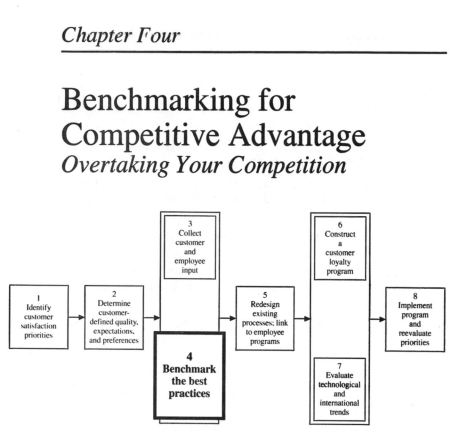

Do as adversaries do in law—strive mightily, but eat and drink as friends.

Shakespeare, *The Taming of the Shrew*

In a utopian view of the world, the European Community would look like the following: The French would be the chefs; the Italians would be the lovers; the Germans would be the mechanics; the English would be the police; and the Swiss would organize everyone.

In a less-than-desirable scenario, the European Community would look different: The French would be the mechanics; the Germans would be the police; the Swiss would be the lovers; the English would be the chefs; and the Italians would organize everything.

Companies, like countries, are known for certain products, services, or areas of expertise. They also fail when they pretend to be something they're not. Competitive advantage is important and must be simple and clear. Customers have little time or interest in remembering details about a product or service. A company that tries to be too many things at once confuses the customer.

Smart companies rarely have trouble naming their competitive advantage:

- "Our product is unique."
- "We're the low-cost producer, so we have the best price."
- "Our customer service is the model for the industry."

However, ask a group of service industry managers how they compete and most would respond, "On service". Press them further and they might add, "value for the dollar," "our people are the key," "convenience," or even "quality." For some firms, these seemingly vague labels actually represent well-informed and successful competitive positioning strategies. But for many others, competitive strategies are dangerously artificial because they are often based on inaccurate or incomplete competitor information.

Many companies assume they know enough about their competition because (1) they know the competitive environment—they live it day to day; and (2) they make some attempt to stay current, for example, by reading trade publications. Companies with active customer research programs can also be lulled into thinking they have sufficient market information. But customer feedback, even when collected properly (Chapter 3), represents only current customers and doesn't provide information about other buyers in the market. Questionnaires don't provide sufficient detail about how things could be done and can't provide an objective perspective of where the company stands. Although focus groups can help fill in these gaps, they usually don't involve competitors' customers and can never provide sufficient information about the operations of competitors.

An approach, new to most U.S. companies, that focuses on keeping or achieving competitive advantage is *benchmarking*. Benchmarking means, quite literally, "learning from your competitors." This is very different from the more traditional, "build a better mousetrap" approach to secure competitive advantage.

*U*sed by themselves, customer and employee surveys can present a limited viewpoint and don't provide enough information for a candid appraisal of where your company stands. Benchmarking provides the missing link that allows businesses to focus on achieving competitive advantage by learning from other companies.

Benchmarking is an important tool. It can lead to useful and highly competitive methods without excessive expenditures. It is intended to identify the best practices available for the sole purpose of improving weaknesses within your organization. But it is only one perspective and should be considered along with your previous findings (Step 5 in Chapter 8 integrates customer, employee, and competitor information).

*B*enchmarking is "the practice of being humble enough to admit that someone else is better at something, and being wise enough to try to learn how to match and even surpass them at it."[1]

THE BENCHMARKING PROCESS

In its simplest form, benchmarking consists of understanding and analyzing a company's procedures and performance in a specific process; finding other departments and companies to determine which is best at a given process; collecting and sharing information about this process; and analyzing the data to see what portions of the other companies' methods can be used by your own company (Exhibit 4–1).

Let's look at these steps in more detail.

Identify a Process Needing Improvement

OK, you get a note from your boss saying how wonderful this thing called benchmarking is and she asks you to take charge of it. The first step, identifying what is to be benchmarked, is the most difficult.

You have begun this self-analysis through the development of the customer and production cycles (refer to Chapter 3). The trick is to figure out

EXHIBIT 4–1
The Competitive Benchmarking Process

1. Identify a process that needs improvement.
2. Measure this process in terms of cost, quality, and time.
3. Search for industrywide best practices to ensure superiority rather than parity.
4. From these, select a benchmarking partner that fits your situation. Be prepared to discuss equivalent internal data and information about your operations.
5. Collect data on this company's processes through surveys, site visits, or consultants. Use the same measures associated with your processes.
6. Identify the gap between this leader and you.
7. Project future performance levels.
8. Integrate benchmarking findings with customer satisfaction strategy.

what your core processes are (a *process* links related tasks to yield a product or service to a customer) and which need improvement. Processes run from start to finish. For example:

Product development: Concept to prototype.
Sales: Prospect to order.
Order fulfillment: Order to payment.
Service: Inquiry to resolution.[2]

Don't benchmark the sales or accounting department, benchmark the work that the people do in those departments. If several of your own processes clearly need improvement, look at each one and identify those that affect your business most. Select the process that has the greatest potential of providing additional value to customers. You might get some hints from focus group results (Chapter 3).

Measure the Process

The essential ingredient to any benchmarking effort is the ability to compare the selected process with that of competitors. This depends on measurement. For example, if you were simply to identify billing as the process for benchmarking, what would you compare? Comparisons are not possible without first measuring your own process. Measurements should include cost, quality, and time. Without these measures you couldn't answer the question, "Why do you need to benchmark the billing process?"

However, by identifying the *costs* of the billing process (e.g., labor, materials, overhead), the *quality* of the service (average percentage of past-due receivables), and the *time* involved (average time between bills sent out and collections received), specific comparisons with competitors can be made.

Perhaps you will identify selling (not the sales department) as your benchmarking subject. Benchmarking how sales are achieved could focus on the following:

- Organizational structure of the sales department.
- Communications with customers and employees.
- Recruitment of top-notch sales reps.
- Motivation and compensation of sales reps.
- Performance measurement methods.
- Training.

You must understand and be able to measure your own sales process before seeking a partner to benchmark. You should be able to measure *performance* (e.g., generating sales leads) and *procedures* contributing to this performance (type and cost of incentive programs or hours invested per lead). Again, focus on the outcome and on the steps necessary to complete the process. Each of these areas may be measured according to cost, quality, and time.

Although the subject for benchmarking should be crystal clear (e.g., guest check-in process, delivering employee health care, or recruiting top-notch sales reps), the benchmarking objective should be general. Don't limit the learning potential. For example, in Ford's quest to reduce the number of employees in its accounts payable department by 20 percent, it found that Mazda had a much smaller staff, about 80 percent smaller. Through benchmarking efforts with Mazda, Ford was able to reduce its staff by 75 percent. In the days before benchmarking, Ford would simply have made an internal study and decided that maybe a 5 percent or 10 percent cut would suffice. But when a company finds that another company is twice as good as it is, or in this case, 50 times as good, it can't just chug along making minor improvements.

Search for Industry Best Practices

The focus is on achieving superior performance. Look at other departments and companies to determine which is really the best performer (see, for example, Exhibit 4–2).

EXHIBIT 4–2

Recognized U.S. Leaders in a Variety of Disciplines

Processes	Leaders
Benchmarking methods	AT&T, Digital Equipment, Ford, IBM, Motorola, Texas Instruments, Xerox
Customer satisfaction	L.L. Bean, Federal Express, GE Plastics, Xerox, Milliken, Maryland Bank–North America (MBNA)
Billing and equipment	American Express, MCI, Fidelity Investments
Distribution and logistics	L.L. Bean, Wal-Mart
Employee empowerment	Corning, Dow, Milliken, Toledo Scale
Equipment maintenance	Disney
Flexible manufacturing	Allen-Bradley, Baldor, Motorola
Health care programs	Allied-Signal, Coors
Marketing	Procter & Gamble
Product Development	Beckman Instruments, Calcomp, NCR, Cincinnati Milacron, DEC, Hewlett-Packard, 3M, Motorola
Quality methods	AT&T, IBM, Motorola, Westinghouse, Xerox
Supplier management	Bose, Ford, Levi Strauss, 3M, Motorola, Xerox
Worker training	Disney, General Electric, Federal Express, Ford

Source: *Business Week*, November 30, 1992, pp. 74–75.

The scope of the search should include one's own company, industry, and companies outside one's industry. This view will ensure superiority rather than parity.

 Select a benchmarking partner from your own company, industry, or outside your industry to ensure superiority rather than parity.

Remember, the focus is on performance. Once you understand your own procedures and performance in a given process, find another company that excels in this area, the top performer.

 Service Wars
Ritz-Carlton Hotels will study the best company in any industry. For example, they benchmarked the topic of "integrating business systems" with previous Baldrige winners from outside the hospitality industry.

Many people think that the quality improvement techniques found in manufacturing can't be transferred to service industries. But whether it's a factory producing products or a hotel providing services, processes depend on methods, materials, and people. In both environments, work is completed by combining these elements, and management must decide where to concentrate its efforts. Manufacturers emphasize machinery and materials; in services, people take precedence.

Although the companies listed in Exhibit 4–2 are among the nation's largest, benchmarking can benefit small companies by helping them copy big-business practices. Listed in Exhibit 4–2 are companies known for benchmarking customer satisfaction. This broad approach is useful when an organization is interested in overall improvement rather than focusing on specific weaknesses. Benchmarking customer satisfaction may lead to additional benchmarking of certain processes needing improvement.

Select several leading examples that are appropriate for your customers and their expectations. Which top performers' procedures are most similar to yours? Contact various benchmarking resources (see Exhibit 4–3) or your own industry association for recommendations on who to benchmark. Read trade publications. Read specialty publications that relate to the process you're benchmarking (e.g., personnel magazines for benchmarking human resource practices). Note the award winners and featured companies. Focus on their strengths and how they compare to your organization.

There are many excellent companies you can benchmark against. Don't spend an inordinate amount of time wrangling over which to pick. An excellent resource to assist with tailoring the benchmark process to your organization is the International Benchmarking Clearinghouse (Exhibit 4–3). Their purpose is to support companies' quality and customer satisfaction efforts by offering a variety of useful benchmarking services. For example, common interest groups meet to discuss a variety of customer satisfaction topics such as complaint handling, how to use survey data, and promoting internal customer satisfaction. Companies skilled in these areas present their experiences to members of the International Benchmarking Clearinghouse (IBC membership costs approximately $6,000 per year). Participants meet with the presenters in breakout groups where they swap ideas and learn more about others' approaches to their problems.

EXHIBIT 4–3
Benchmarking Resources

Organizations
- The International Benchmarking Clearinghouse, Houston, TX, (713) 685-4666. They sell seminars and access to a database of best practices and how-to guidelines. Has about 100 members, paying from $6,000 to $60,000, including the biggest names in American business.
- Strategic Planning Institute (SPI) Council on Benchmarking, Cambridge, MA, (617) 491-9200. About 50 companies have enrolled at $8,000 apiece to attend four conferences annually and to use the council's database of case studies.
- The Big 6 accounting firms are becoming more involved with benchmarking. Best known is Arthur Consulting for its best practices database.
- Best Practices Benchmarking & Consulting Inc., Lexington, MA, (617) 863-9606. A smaller, specialized consulting firm.

Books
- *Benchmarking. The Search for Industry Best Practices That Lead to Superior Performance,* Robert C. Camp (Milwaukee, WI: ASQC Quality Press, 1989). Written by a pioneer of the subject, this is the single best overview of benchmarking.
- *The Benchmarking Book,* Michael J. Spendolini (New York: Amacom Books, 1992). Reviews the lessons learned from early benchmarkers such as Xerox, AT&T, Motorola, IBM, DEC, DuPont, and Boeing.
- *Strategic Benchmarking,* Greg Watson (New York: John Wiley & Sons, 1993).
- For a bibliography of over 100 articles and reports on benchmarking, contact the International Benchmarking Clearinghouse, (713) 681-4320. $25.

Select a Benchmarking Partner

Contact and obtain permission from the prospective partner. Although it is usually preferable to obtain permission and cooperation from another firm, it's not always necessary, as discussed later in this chapter.

L.L. Bean[3] is a recognized world leader in maintaining high levels of customer satisfaction (90 percent of their business is through catalog mail-order sales) and is also known for their superiority in several specific business functions (see Exhibit 4–2). They will *not* agree to benchmark with (1) direct competitors, (2) companies that don't know why they are benchmarking, or (3) companies that aren't willing to reciprocate. They really get turned off by the words, "Our company policy prevents us from . . . "

L.L. Bean will partner with companies that know what they want to benchmark and excel in an area where they (L.L. Bean) could use improvement. Although they value opinions ("we're the recognized leader in . . ."), the potential partner must be able to demonstrate its competency through standard measurements. When organizations as diverse as the U.S. Air Force or the Department of Defense call requesting benchmarking assistance, L.L. Bean asks them what they excel at and how they can confirm this claim. For example, L.L. Bean may ask "Where does your company excel in customer satisfaction?" "What were the highest customer satisfaction scores in your customer survey?" If a company quantifies the process connected to the particular performance area, the other company is more likely to agree to be a benchmarking partner.

Who does L.L. Bean benchmark? It looks for companies that are proficient in a particular process rather than focusing on any particular industry. L.L. Bean has sought out and benchmarked such companies as Milliken, Digital Equipment, and IBM for specific processes they were looking to improve. L.L. Bean benchmarked IBM on how they conduct their own benchmarking process and on how they handle a large volume of benchmarking requests. One important lesson they learned was that IBM considers their benchmarking services part of marketing—everyone is a potential customer of IBM. (For information on IBM's free benchmarking services, call (919) 543-5705, or write IBM Benchmarking, PO Box 12195, Research Triangle Park, NC 27709. For information on benchmarking with L.L. Bean, call (207) 865-4761.)

Acquiring permission and information from an organization may be difficult. But when the objective of this effort is identified as pursuing best practices, the other parties are likely to be interested in understanding the practices that make their operation successful.

Are other organizations truly comparable to yours? Significant differences may result from size. Size may affect the way operations are run. A larger organization may be automated where a smaller one operates manually. It may require additional jobs or even levels of employees. Entire processes may be necessary or disappear because of increases in volume. You may have to adapt or scale their methods to yours. If the organizations differ greatly (for example, a hotel using a manufacturer for inventory management benchmarking), too much time and energy may be required to make the comparisons work.

Remember, the focus is on achieving superior performance—select the performance leaders. Staying within your industry can result in "inbreeding"; you cannot afford to be unaware of developments occurring outside your field. But what if benchmarking does not turn up a new idea? It may be possible that no one in another company has had a great idea that is applicable to your operation. This should not end your benchmarking efforts. Rather, consider it a challenge to create the new world-class benchmark. By continuing to benchmark others, you may pick and choose from the leaders to assemble your own unique process.

Collect Data

The most common and valuable data collection tool in benchmarking is the site visit. There is no substitute for visiting your benchmarking partner. Because site visits are conducted infrequently and may be somewhat awkward given the subject matter, following specific guidelines can increase the chances for success.

Site visit guidelines:

1. Determine the most appropriate person to contact. If the potential benchmarking partner is a supplier or a customer, contact a familiar person or the sales rep or account manager. Ask him or her to assist with arranging the visit.[4] Stress the interest in uncovering industry best practices. If this is done in a professional manner, it should pave the way for mutual benefit through sharing of information.

2. Outline the topic areas of interest to serve as a guide for the visit.

3. Ensure that the performance and procedures in your equivalent internal operation is understood and is documented in measurable terms.

4. Obtain and review all available relevant data on the company in advance.

5. Prepare a list of questions covering:
   a. Best practices, current or planned.
   b. Measures, including cost (of inputs), quality, and time (of outputs).

6. Establish a team of three people directly related to the process being investigated. Three is the best size: one asks questions, one notes the answers, and the third thinks of the next question. Conduct the interview methodically and gather all relevant data and information.

7. Retain important points and ask for clarification after the site visit. A small cassette recorder, used with permission, is useful for a debriefing meeting to be held after the site visit. Clarify

Information and plan for follow-up methods to obtain missing information.

8. Be prepared to discuss your equivalent internal data and, if necessary, additional information. Offer a reciprocal visit and tour if appropriate.

9. Debrief team members as quickly as possible following the tour. The discussion should cover general observations as well as information received.

10. Document the tour in a written report. Thank the benchmarking partner for their time and cooperation in person and in writing.

 *B*e prepared to discuss your equivalent internal data and, if necessary, information about other processes in your operations. The real gains for both sides come from improvements in procedure and in streamlining current processes.

Identify the Gap

By comparing industry leader strengths and your performance, you will find a positive performance gap, a negative performance gap, or parity. A positive gap should receive appropriate recognition, but this finding is unlikely because of your selection criteria. Parity is also unlikely. However, benchmarking is typically restricted to a point in time. So a parity position may exist but be short-lived. It may also be an inaccurate reading of the situation and may be explained by unusually performing processes.

Focus on the negative gap because it represents the real improvement opportunity. Analyze the data collected about your company's partner's process to see what methods it uses that would help close the gap for you. This includes improved knowledge, practices, and processes.

When Xerox focused on the improvement of their order fulfillment process, they benchmarked L.L. Bean. Although the two companies are in very different businesses, both needed to handle products that varied considerably in size and shape. By learning and implementing L.L. Bean's "picking" process, Xerox reduced their warehousing costs by 10 percent.[5]

EXHIBIT 4-4
Benchmarking the Future: Accounts Payable Labor Cost

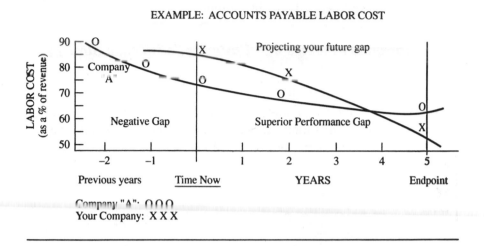

EXAMPLE: ACCOUNTS PAYABLE LABOR COST

Company "A": O O O
Your Company: X X X

Project Future Performance Levels

So far we have defined where you and your partner are today. But competitors continue to pursue improvements. Therefore, it is necessary to project where you, your benchmarking partner, and your gap (+ or −) are likely to be in the future.

For example, if you were benchmarking company A's accounts payable process, labor cost would likely be a critical measurement to obtain. This is called a *metric* in benchmarking language. These metrics are most often used in the form of percent of revenue. Refer to Exhibit 4-4. Company A's labor cost, as a percent of sales, is currently 75 percent. Your labor cost is 77 percent, so a 2 percent gap currently exists between this leader and you. By assuming a continuing rate of improvement plus any stated plans for change, you can estimate a future benchmark. Last year's labor cost for company A was 80 percent, as shown in the exhibit, down from the previous year's 82 percent. The company also plans to automate one function over the next several years, reducing labor cost by another 3 percent. Company A will likely reduce their labor cost by a total of 5 percent in two years, aiming for the 70 percent level. Following this pattern, future levels may be estimated. Remember, you are predicting the future here, so it will be an approximation.

By benchmarking the current and expected future leader, you can select a course of action that will allow you to reach and overtake the projected leading level. This will be the focus of the next chapter: how to redesign a process to achieve a desired goal in the future.

Integrate Findings with Customer Satisfaction Strategy

Great care must be taken to position benchmarking relative to your customer satisfaction efforts. It must be successfully integrated into your operation. This requires the understanding that benchmarking is not just another program of the month. It is a tactical weapon that contributes to the customer satisfaction mission, a valuable tool that should be used over and over again.

LOW-PROFILE BENCHMARKING WITHOUT PERMISSION

Information gathering is vital to the competitive process and can be done ethically and legally *without* the cooperation of a benchmarking partner. Detailed competitor information is becoming more readily available. Various informal approaches to gathering information can be useful for small-scale competitor research and do not require the cooperation of a benchmarking partner.

Competitive intelligence can be gathered through various internal sources. Employees, especially salespeople, hear a lot about their competitors. Customers and suppliers can keep the company informed about competitors and their products through focus groups and other discussions. Customers often use experience with competitors to shape their evaluations of your product or service. They have different levels of experience and knowledge of the competition—but this view, whatever it is, is critical. How the customer perceives your product or service, especially with regard to expectations and quality, includes valuable competitor information. Use questions focusing on competitor performance. Compare these findings to similar measures of your own performance.

Spotters can also provide information on competitors. How quickly does the competition answer the phone, deliver room service, or respond to a complaint? Who are your competitors' suppliers. How often do they receive delivery? Actually trying a competitor's services can strengthen your operational processes and procedures. Target particular areas lacking in your operation. For example, if special requests are a source of complaints for your business, make a special order from a competitor, asking enough questions to have them explain their entire fulfillment procedure. Evaluate the pros and cons as a customer would.

External sources are also helpful in gathering competitor information. Published materials, from want ads to relevant association and trade journals, are useful. Government sources[6] such as local zoning and tax assessment offices often have tax information on local stores and even blueprints of the facility, showing square footage and other layout details, all publicly available.

Another source of low-profile benchmarking is commercial data. Outside suppliers such as A.C. Nielsen Company and the Market Research Corporation of America provide helpful information. In addition, more than 3,000 databases exist. For example, Adtrack tracks ads in 150 consumer and business publications, providing information by which to assess competitors ad strategies and styles.

Low-profile benchmarking avoids giving away information about your own strengths and weaknesses. You may also gain valuable insights not available in a cooperative venture. Although companies should consider intelligence gathering an acceptable and necessary practice, companies do not have to break the law or accepted codes of ethics to get good information, as shown in Exhibit 4–5.

Just as world-class companies are responsive to the customers' viewpoint, observing and acting on information about competitors should be taken seriously. Benchmarking is an essential tool for staying competitive, improving current operations, and maximizing customer satisfaction.

Benchmarking is often done in conjunction with redesign efforts: rethinking work flow and the procedures used to perform various tasks. This is discussed in Step 5 in Chapter 8.

SUMMARY

- Used by themselves, customer and employee surveys can present a limited viewpoint and don't provide enough information for a candid appraisal of where your company stands. Benchmarking

EXIIIBIT 4–5
Ethics of Benchmarking

Good practices

- Gathering information directly from other companies with their consent; from other primary sources (e.g., buying competitive products on the market, trade shows); from secondary sources (e.g., public documents); from your customers; and from your employees.

- Contacting a lawyer when an information-gathering practice appears questionable.

- Obtaining all necessary clearances in advance if confidential information is to be shared.

- Avoiding the search for specific information on prices, pricing policies, marketing strategies, marketplace activities, and consumer information.[7]

Bad practices

- Trespassing on another company's property with the intent to collect information.

- Bribing individuals to act as informants.

- Bugging or eavesdropping on another company's privileged or private communications.

- Learning, even inadvertently, about a competitor's pricing considerations.

- Trading in the stock in a company after learning about material information that hasn't been publicly disclosed.

- Requiring suppliers to participate in a benchmarking study as a condition of obtaining or keeping your business.

Questionable practices—Things to avoid

- Recruiting employees from competing companies for the purpose of obtaining information.

- Asking questions at technical meetings without identifying your company and name.

- Subscribing to competitors' technical journals or attending user conferences as a private individual without disclosing your corporate affiliation.

- Talking about information obtained from one organization while visiting another.

- Giving information in a public forum about a benchmarking partner without its permission.

- Asking for information you wouldn't provide yourself.

- Visiting or soliciting information from a benchmarking partner without first understanding your own processes.

- During a site visit, requesting last minute changes or additions to the agenda to gain addition access to the company's information.

Source: International Benchmarking Clearinghouse, Houston, TX.

provides the missing link that allows businesses to focus on achieving competitive advantage by learning from other companies.

- Benchmarking is "the practice of being humble enough to admit that someone else is better at something and being wise enough to try to learn how to match and even surpass them at it."

- Select a benchmarking partner from your own company, industry, or outside your industry to ensure superiority rather than parity.

- Be prepared to discuss your equivalent internal data and, if necessary, information about other processes in your operations. The real gains for both sides come from improvements in procedure and in streamlining current processes.

NOTES

1. Marion Harmon, "Benchmarking," *Quality Digest* 7, no. 2 (July, 19 1991), p 20.
2. M. Hammer and J. Champy, *Reengineering the Corporation: A Manifesto for Business Revolution* (New York: Harper Business, 1993), p. 118.
3. Based on a conversation with Barry Kinner, benchmarking consultant, L.L. Bean, Freeport, ME, on August 25, 1993.
4. This should be a free visit. Some companies charge a fee for their time, especially previous Baldrige winners. The Ritz-Carlton Hotel Company, for example, charges $200 per person for their "Quality Site Visits" (staying overnight is extra).
5. Otis Port and Geoffrey Smith, "Beg, Borrow—And Benchmark" *Business Week*, November 30, 1992, p. 74.
6. See "The Federal Government Is a Treasure Trove of Valuable, Free Data for the Marketing Researcher," *Marketing News*, August 19, 1983, p. 10. For example, the government sells the results of a $100,000 study of the fast-food industry for only 25 cents.
7. Robert C. Camp, *Benchmarking: The Search for Industry Best Practices That Lead to Superior Performance*, (Milwaukee, WI: ASQC Quality Press, 1989), p. 117.

Chapter Five

Designing World-Class Customer Satisfaction
Achieving an Outward Customer Orientation

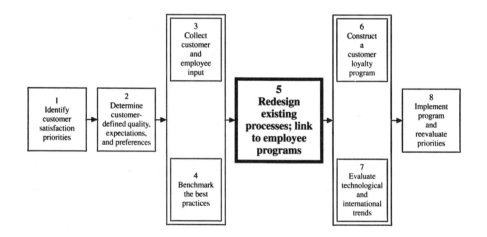

Always design a thing by considering it in its larger context—a chair in a room, a room in a house, a house in an environment in a city plan.

Eliel Saarinen, *Architect and Designer*

U. S. business has begun to understand the concept of customer satisfaction but has difficulty translating this knowledge into daily operations. Understanding the concept is different than knowing what should be done, deciding how to do it, or actually doing it. We'll first discuss how to redesign elements of your customer process using a combination of customer, employee, and competitor input. Second, we'll review the latest approaches to employee management that can support the delivery of your newly designed process.

REDESIGNING PROCESSES

Managers often know what has to be improved. Take bank service, for example. Most banks know that customer satisfaction would improve if they could make customers feel less intimidated and more knowledgeable about what they offer, for instance, by using a more understandable pricing structure. But how would a bank manager approach this?

The objective would be to modify the elements contributing to dissatisfaction (poor customer information and confusing pricing), add ingredients to enhance satisfaction (superior customer handling and customer-friendly pricing), and combine them into a new presentation of customer-valued products and services, including a streamlined customer experience. Removing the barriers to customer satisfaction (see Chapter 1) is what redesign is all about. This involves reshaping products and bureaucratic procedures, adopting technology, and addressing managerial roadblocks, and personnel and cost issues. Using customer, employee, and competitor information, the objective is to redesign existing processes to offer maximum customer benefits with organizational effectiveness.

A large-scale approach to promoting change for the purpose of improving customer satisfaction is *reengineering*, one of the most significant management concepts since the quality movement.[1] In this approach, employees look outward toward the customer to satisfy their needs instead of looking inward toward their boss to comply with his or her demands.[2] The concept assumes that most companies are organized inefficiently because they're focused on specialists working in functional islands such as accounting or marketing. It's also based on the idea that organizations are made up of processes, series of activities that deliver products and services to customers.[3] Reengineering focuses on the internal processes necessary to support specific steps in the customer experience. Customer processes are the service portions of the complete customer service cycle.

*P*rocesses are related tasks that provide a product or service to customers. Organize improvement efforts around these customer-driven processes (the service side of the customer service cycle), not around departments such as sales or production.

For example, guests checking into a hotel are part of the arrival process (airport transportation, baggage handling, hotel reception/check-in, and settling into a room). Similarly, the series of events necessary to prepare a hotel room qualify as a process.

Reengineering requires companies to create new ways of handling basic products and services. These efforts often reorganize fundamental elements of the work process. The principles of reengineering, however, do not have to be carried to an extreme to be effective. For example, IBM Credit Corp. used to take six days to approve a loan application, although it took only 90 minutes of actual work. But the company redesigned the approval process. Instead of having the application passed around to three or four different people, each from a separate function such as credit, sales, or accounting, it reorganized the process by assigning a single person to perform all the necessary functions. Now, one person handles each application in less than four hours.

*U*sing customer, employee, and competitor information, remove barriers to satisfaction by redesigning existing processes.

Hallmark Cards provides another example of redesigning a single process. The company was surprisingly slow in getting new greeting cards from concept to market; it took two to three years. Hallmark discovered that during 90 percent of this "development" time, the work sat in someone's in or out basket, being passed around to 25 different people. The company redesigned the development process and now gets new lines out within one year.

Organizations needing to become more customer responsive will likely benefit from some reengineering efforts. Most companies, however, are not completely inefficient or ineffective with their current structure and processes. For these companies, a moderate approach (as opposed to an all-or-nothing approach) focusing on individual processes and unmet customer needs may be effective and can address a wide spectrum of problems.

The process of improving the customer experience will differ for each situation because it must be tailored to diverse customers' needs. There is no recipe for devising new ways of servicing customers or modifying current approaches that will guarantee an improved customer experience in all situations. The steps we will use to improve customer processes are general but are based on specific information you have gathered. The redesign steps are as follows:

1. Focus on the problem.
2. Identify causes.
3. Consider alternative courses of action.
4. Redesign for customer satisfaction.

Adapt these steps to your situation by using the detailed approach presented in Step 5 of the World-Class Customer Satisfaction Program.

Focus on the Problem

By keeping in mind your original objective (refer to Chapter 1) and listening to customers, employees, and competitors (Chapters 2–4), you should learn which processes are clearly not working or need improvement. The key is to focus on those that present the highest potential for improvement. By linking these weak processes to internal barriers to customer satisfaction (Chapter 1), you can identify problem areas.

For example, the general manager at Hotel X conducted a guest survey based on a typical customer cycle (Chapter 1). Analyzing the components of this cycle (Chapter 2), he found that room service received the lowest customer satisfaction score (Chapter 3). He conducted several focus groups to further understand customer needs relating to room service and to consider employee input. Customers agreed on a customer service cycle that represented their previous room service experience and employees agreed on the current service side of the cycle (Exhibit 5–1).

In focus group discussions with customer and employees, various issues surfaced: late-night orders received by the switchboard operator were sent to one person in the kitchen who had to answer the telephone and prepare items; shortages of ingredients were common; all three delivery carts were run-down; several competitors were known for providing

EXHIBIT 5–1
Room Service Customer Service Cycle

Customer perspective
1. Guest calls room service.
2. Places order.
3. Answers door; talks with server; signs bill.
4. Consumes food and beverage.
5. Sets tray outside door for pickup.
6. Reviews room service charges at check-out.

Hotel perspective
1–2. Switchboard staff trained for order taking.
3. Staff trained on the job in service techniques; uniforms required.
4. Kitchen staff instructed on consistent preparation of all menu items.
5. Housekeeping coordinated with room service staff for timely pickup of trays.
6. Charges posted on guest's hotel bill.

superior room service. Other problems identified by customers and employees included delivery of wrong orders, which added to delays; unpleasant servers, and poor food quality.

Armed with the above details, the manager wanted to see how his hotel's room service procedure stacked up against that of the competition. He and the food and beverage manager benchmarked (Chapter 4) several competitors known for excelling at room service. Their goal was to find ways to improve their own process. They also benchmarked a fast-food pizza parlor known for its speedy service and hot deliveries. Compared to the competitor hotels, their biggest negative gap was the cycle time, that is, guests had to wait longer in their hotel because of various manual procedures. The competitors' best practices averaged 18 minutes; Hotel X's current average was 48 minutes. They also learned how to keep food hot from observing the pizza operation.

Their next step was to find the cause of their difficulties.

Identify Causes

A fishbone analysis is a management tool that helps to uncover the root causes of a problem based on internal barriers to customer satisfaction. The managers at Hotel X selected this technique to examine possible explanations for their problem because it combined customer, competitor,

EXHIBIT 5–2
Fishbone Analysis of Poor Room Service

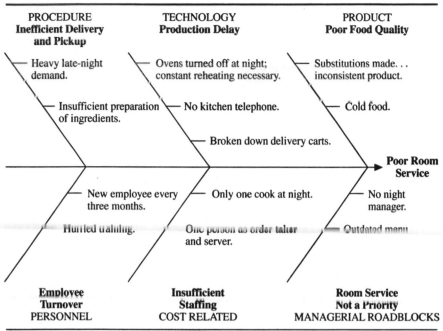

PROCEDURE Inefficient Delivery and Pickup	TECHNOLOGY Production Delay	PRODUCT Poor Food Quality
Heavy late-night demand.	Ovens turned off at night; constant reheating necessary.	Substitutions made... inconsistent product.
Insufficient preparation of ingredients.	No kitchen telephone.	Cold food.
	Broken down delivery carts.	→ Poor Room Service
New employee every three months.	Only one cook at night.	No night manager.
Hurried training.	One person as order taker and server.	Outdated menu
Employee Turnover PERSONNEL	**Insufficient Staffing** COST RELATED	**Room Service Not a Priority** MANAGERIAL ROADBLOCKS

Note: Each branch focuses on a single barrier to customer satisfaction.

and employee perspectives in a simple format. Exhibit 5–2 diagrams their fishbone analysis.

Complaints about room service are explained by six contributing factors: Inefficient delivery and pickup, production delays, poor food quality, employee turnover, insufficient staffing, and inadequate management attention. Fishbone analysis allows a company to break down a large problem to focus on its underlying causes. Classifying the causes helps to isolate the areas responsible for the poor service and thus facilitates correction.

Service Wars
The redesign of the hotel check-in process has been made possible with new technology. The often burdensome check-in procedure can now be completed efficiently by employees using handheld computers. For some hotels, this "mobile front desk" accommodates guests in hotel lobbies, in hotel vans, or even at baggage claim areas in airports.[4]

EXHIBIT 5-3
Removing Internal Barriers to Customer Satisfaction

Barrier	Action
Product	Involve customer and employee in product development process.
Personnel	Consider employee involvement and other best practices in human resource management.
Bureaucratic	Reduce amount of steps in process.
Technology	Evaluate customer benefits of new technology.
Managerial	Refocus on customer priorities.
Cost-related	Benchmark low-cost leaders.

Consider Alternative Courses of Action

The managers considered what could be done to eliminate these obstacles, as shown in Exhibit 5–3. They decided that the food and beverage manager would come up with alternatives to address the product and cost-related barriers and that his assistant manager would come up with options to solve the problems located on the remaining branches.

On the basis of customer and employee suggestions to make the whole process more customer friendly, the food and beverage manager offered various options: (1) allow outside, fast-food businesses to deliver to the guest rooms, and charge a fee to these companies; (2) commit larger staffs to room service; (3) streamline procedures that relate to processing and delivering orders to guests; and (4) purchase equipment to reduce preparation and delivery time, including new carts with improved heating and holding capabilities. The general manager considered each of these as realistic alternatives to improving their room service.

Redesign for Customer Satisfaction

After conducting the fishbone analysis (rooting out and prioritizing the problems contributing to poor room service), evaluating the various suggestions on how to address these issues, and benchmarking superior competitor practices, the managers redesigned the customer service cycle.

The major changes included directing all room service calls into the kitchen with a designated phone line, eliminating the separate step of calling orders into the kitchen; cross-training kitchen staff in several areas of room service such as order taking and preparation of ingredients; creating new standards to ensure that there would be enough food in stock and preprepared when appropriate; placing two room service buttons on guest room phones (one to call the hotel kitchen, the other to call a nearby franchise pizza delivery service that agreed to serve the hotel); adding one more person to the kitchen night staff during peak hours; installing improved heating elements on delivery carts; creating a separate room service employee training program (none had existed before); and, sweeping halls more frequently to remove trays. The managers also established a procedure for updating the menu based on item popularity and created new standards for improving delivery time (six months after improvements were implemented, an 18 minute average would be expected).

Despite all of these improvements, prices would have to remain competitive given the new fast-food competition. The goal was to provide a high-quality product with very prompt service. Exhibit 5–4 presents the redesigned room service process (compare with Exhibit 5–1).

The general manager realized that the ultimate test would be customers' response to the new services. After consulting with other managers, he instituted a bonus system based on guest satisfaction ratings of room service. Although the total payouts would be relatively low at first, the incentive to please guests would affect the entire process and support his redesign efforts.

This room service example demonstrates how by separately addressing its underlying causes, a complex problem can be confronted. The general manager removed the internal barriers contributing to guest complaints as follows:

- Personnel—Cross-training and bonus system increased employee involvement.
- Bureaucratic—Order-processing steps were reduced.
- Technology—Changes to the phone system benefited guests.
- Managerial—Resource commitments indicated shift of priorities.
- Cost-related—Low-cost pizza alternative adapted.

EXHIBIT 5–4
Redesigned Room Service Customer Service Cycle

Customer perspective

1. Guest calls room service using speed-dialing preset button.
2. Places order.
3. Answers door; talks with server; signs bill.
4. Consumes food and beverage.
5. Sets tray outside door for pickup.
6. Reviews room service charges at checkout.

Hotel perspective

1. Phone rings in kitchen.
2. Call answered by staff trained for room service order taking. Kitchen staff instructed on consistent preparation of all menu items. New standards ensure adequate purchase and preparation of items to prevent stock-outs.
3. Staff formally trained in room service delivery techniques; superior uniform presentation, and upkeep, and quick delivery is required.
4. All food delivered at proper temperatures, ensured by proper equipment.
5. Room service staff notes room number and delivery time to ensure prompt tray pickup (timing of hallway sweep).
6. Charges are posted to guest's hotel bill, which is immediately accessible through guest's TV.

Although all of these changes streamlined and improved the guest experience, the use of employee feedback and the attention given to employee issues were especially critical in the redesign process. The key is to set up employee programs that will strengthen current and re-designed customer processes.

EMPLOYEE MANAGEMENT—FINDING BEST SOLUTIONS

In many organizations, management treats employees as unvalued and unintelligent. The employees, in turn, convey the identical message to the customer. It is the rare employee who can rise above the effects of such poor management.[5]

*E*mployees treat customers similar to the way they, as employees, are treated by management.

Although many businesses realize this connection, the lingering effects of changing owners, obsolete management styles, and outmoded employee programs have restricted attempts to increase worker productivity. Firms must be willing to try new management approaches not only to rid themselves of prior constraints, but also to keep up with operational changes (redesign) occurring within the company.

 *S*electing the right employee program can add considerable strength to the design and delivery of your customer processes.

In the room service example, the redesign improved the process. This included creating new standards for ordering, preparation, and delivery (time and procedures); adopting new equipment; retraining the kitchen and housekeeping staffs; and implementing a new bonus system. Virtually all of these modifications depend on the cooperation of employees. Without effective programs that focus on the current demands placed on employees, the redesign effort will likely fail and cause additional damage. The challenge is to facilitate these changes and support the new process with appropriate employee programs.

For customer satisfaction efforts to succeed, the organization must reinvent and rejuvenate its human resource (HR) programs through internal partnerships, communication with employees, and self-monitoring. Cadillac developed cross-functional, people-strategy teams to research, design, implement, and evaluate various HR programs.

This section does not discuss the usual inward-looking approach to managing human resources. We are interested in how employees affect customer satisfaction. Our primary concern is not how to reduce labor costs or even how to improve service quality. We are only concerned with those approaches to employee management that significantly affect the customer and contribute to the success of the redesign process.

At a meeting of four presidents of leading hotel companies, the topic was the future of their industry. One president emphasized the social changes occurring across the country and how these would affect travel.

The second executive pointed to technology as having the biggest impact on business and thus requiring the most attention. The third emphasized financing issues related to real estate and money markets. The fourth was discouraged, pointing out that no one had mentioned the customer or the employee. He compared this to car company executives not talking about their automobiles—"Ridiculous!" He explained that employees are their principal product and that the key issue facing them in the 90s was to get their employees to feel more a part of their organization. He continued,

> Rather than simply performing a function, like these chairs we're sitting in are doing, we have to ask more of our employees. Employees need to feel compassion for their work. They are motivated as much by their hearts and minds as by their pocketbooks. It's unjust to ask or expect employees to function like a chair. Each employee should feel the self-worth that comes from creating and being a part of a vision of serving customers."[6]

World-class companies stand for something worthwhile and communicate this vision to employees with passion. General Electric's vision of a customer-focused organization is conveyed by their "workout" program. This approach, based on a passion for quality and emphasis of trust and confidence among employees, has achieved radical breakthroughs in products and services. At Southwest Airlines the vision is productivity, fun, and working together as a family.

 Creating a passionate and motivated workforce starts with a vision for the organization. Visions should be simple, communicated at every opportunity, and personally conveyed by top management. Create a human resources vision statement embodying the ideal spirit of your organization.

All human resource efforts must start with a vision. An idea that communicates imagination and foresight can contribute to employee commitment and enthusiasm. But conviction must be framed in real programs to offer practical guidance for employees.

Employees feel part of the organization's vision and grow in an environment that encourages personal commitment and development. This dedication can be achieved by selecting those approaches that best fit your organization. All employee-directed activities, from recruitment to retirement, should be firmly grounded in a vision statement. New programs

EXHIBIT 5-5
Residence Inn Vision Statement

Residence Inn will exceed the expectations of every guest, every day, every stay.

This vision depends on us—we are the foundation of this business and we work for Residence Inn because we love it!

We will:

* Celebrate and reward commitment.
* Foster teamwork, ethics, and high expectations.
* Build mutual respect, trust, and friendship.
* Respect the balance of work and home.
* Provide opportunities to learn, grow, succeed, and have fun.

We will operate Residence Inn at a profit, consistently delivering attractive returns to investors, and thereby providing vitality and growth for the system.

We will constantly improve our systems, practices, and capabilities to ensure that the Residence name continues to mean the *best* in the lodging business.

At Residence Inn we want the best product and the best people, caring for our guests and caring for each other.

Source: Residence Inn by Marriott.

should be identified with the established, shared vision of the organization. Exhibit 5–5 presents such a vision statement.

Despite a well-defined vision, many organizations are confronted with hurdles that restrict employees from performing processes, current and redesigned, as they were intended. We will identify the most widespread employee-related issues contributing to this interference and recommend employee programs that can address the causes and effects of these problems.

THE ISSUES

According to Daryl Hartley-Leonard, president of Hyatt Hotel Corporation, the keys to affecting customer satisfaction through human resource management in the 1990s will be:

* Communicating and building relationships with employees; being honest and forthcoming well in advance of any necessary staff or other reductions.

- Empowering employees to let them do what they do best. Reduce cumbersome layers of arrogant managers—employees get their poor attitude from poor management. Ninety-nine percent of employees want to do a good job, to be positive, friendly, and sincere.
- Managing the new social legislation; financially coping with the effects of ADA (the disabilities act), OSHA (safety regulations), and managed health care.[7]

Other industry pacesetters agree. Stan Bromley, regional vice president of Four Season's Hotels, believes that relationship building with employees will be critical to improving customer satisfaction. Jonathan Tisch, president of Loews Hotels, affirms that successful employee programs must be tailored to the needs of the individual. Although difficult economic conditions will persist, he believes that certain exceptional approaches, such as their community outreach policy, create an environment conducive to service and are worth the extra effort and expense.[8]

The issues identified by these executives represent the major problems plaguing many service and manufacturing industries. These problems include high-turnover, unsatisfactory service quality, and not enough skilled workers.

The primary task in any redesign effort is to select appropriate employee programs to address the issues confronting the organization. We'll look at how world-class companies successfully deal with these difficulties. These best solutions, as presented in Exhibit 5–6, focus on three goals: increasing employee loyalty, improving productivity, and encouraging professional and personal development.

Increasing Employee Loyalty

Employee loyalty is a precious commodity. Beyond the costs of bringing a new employee on board and up to speed, service businesses demand a continuity of service. They depend on employees knowing their customers, knowing the new technology, and even taking risks on behalf of customers when necessary. This requires time. Constantly changing faces that customers and employees have to get used to can be more than just inconvenient.

Although many U.S. firms have developed their own approaches to improved quality and productivity and are coping with changing labor demands, they have a long way to go in managing their most important resource, labor. The American workforce is not known for its allegiance. Employee loyalty is at an all-time low.[9] The entire hourly workforce of hotels is replaced each and every year, a 100 percent turnover. Other service industries experience over 200 percent annual turnover rates of their hourly employees.

Why do employees quit? Workers often see their current job as a springboard for their next, perhaps with a competitor. Increased competition has required downsizing of the workforce and is responsible for other financial cutbacks (e.g., reduced profit sharing, stock programs, and stricter controls of supplies and fringe benefits). These changes make employees wary. But the principal reason workers leave jobs is that they lack incentives to stay. Their needs are not being met: they are not recognized sufficiently and often have little opportunity for a career path.

There always is a best approach to one employee's problem, but this solution will not work for everyone. Just as products and services may be tailored to an individual customer's needs, finding personal solutions to employee problems is possible and more effective than standardized human resource programs and policies. Exhibit 5–6 presents a menu of approaches to solving complex employee problems.

 *J*ust as products and services may be tailored to individual customer needs, a company's personnel issues can be more effectively addressed through customized programs and strategies.

In July 1993, Clinton held a workplace summit in Chicago for 200 companies that involve workers in daily decision making. According to the U.S. secretary of labor Robert B. Reich, "There is no way to create a competitive (international) advantage other than through people. Firms are discovering slowly that highly motivated and skilled employees are the key to long-term profitability."

A leader in this movement is General Mills. Its plant in Lodi, California, is a showcase for the company's employee involvement (EI) programs. Called *shared control,* this program eliminated three levels of management, created worker teams, and gave production and quality responsibilities to the workers. Previously, an absent person's work would remain untouched until he or she returned. Now, others will help out. These groups have been trained to perform a "business mission for

EXHIBIT 5–6
The Best Solutions Model

Common Problems	Goals	Best Solutions
High turnover	Loyalty	Quality recruitment and meaningful orientation
		Ongoing training and development
		Realistic career opportunities (career pathing)
		Work-life programs
		Long-term incentive and reward systems
Low productivity	Quality	Employee involvement (EI) teams
		TQM programs
		Motivation empowerment, through enfranchisement, and pay for performance
Insufficient knowledge	Professional and personal development	Training and education
		Cross-training
		Broadbanding

the customer'' and are responsible for all of the attendant concerns such as cost, productivity, and quality.

At this plant, workers dramatically improved quality by confronting customers' most frequent complaint (poor sealing of boxes) and found a remedy for the problem. Workers now say that this ''customer mission'' gives them a greater feeling of accomplishment and job security and motivates them to work harder.

 *E*liminate unnecessary levels of management, create worker teams, and give production and quality responsibilities to employees.

A danger in adopting an EI program is that if it is not implemented sufficiently, it can create new problems. Companies that promise employee participation but then don't change the sources of control and authority in their organization are vulnerable to worker dissatisfaction. When this occurs the next program may be harder to introduce.

EXHIBIT 5–7
Sources for Information on Employee Programs

* Center for Effective Organizations, School of Business, University of Southern California, Los Angeles, CA 90089-1421—Seminars, publications, action research projects. They have a panel of researchers who will take phone calls at 213-743-8765.
* American Society of Training and Development, 1630 Duke St., Box 1443, Alexandria VA 22313—Books, videos, and articles in the field of human resource development.
* American Management Association, 135 West 50th St., New York, NY 10020— Human Resource Division, (212) 903-8020; switchboard, (212) 586-8100.

Implementing an EI program is a complex process because many established practices may be affected. From redesigning reward systems and altering structures of power and authority to changing how information is shared among departments, introducing an EI program requires considerable effort. Companies often reevaluate or even abandon commitments to employee involvement because of initial challenges. But short-term sacrifices are worth the benefits received from involving employees in daily and long-term decision making. For more information on employee programs and the potential pitfalls of them, contact the sources listed in Exhibit 5–7.

According to ongoing research by the Center for Effective Organizations, the majority of the Fortune 1000 companies that practice employee involvement find that support by top management is the most important condition for success.[10] Exhibit 5–8 lists other helpers and barriers to employee involvement as found in their research.

This is hardly surprising. Meaningful change in hierarchical organizations is nearly impossible to achieve without the support of top management. Support by middle management as a condition for success, ranked a distant second. Any EI program will be in danger, however, without support developing from lower levels soon after a program's introduction. More surprising is that offering monetary rewards to employees for their participation does not help to make these programs work. Only 7 percent find success with dollar incentives.

The most common barrier to launching EI programs in Fortune 1,000 companies is short-term performance pressure. Rather than starting an EI program because everyone else is doing it, what's more important is having long-term objectives. EI programs need time to show their real value.

EXHIBIT 5–8
Helpers and Barriers to Employee Involvement

Helpers	Barriers
Support by top management.	Short-term performance pressure
Support by middle management.	Lack of long-term strategy
Availability of resources (money, personnel, etc.) for EI activities	Unclear objectives
Decentralization of authority	Lack of a champion for employee involvement program
Support by first-line managers	Centralization of decisions

Source: Center for Effective Organizations, University of Southern California.

According to these top companies, a lack of technology, knowledge or resources will not restrict EI programs. Instead, companies that are not willing to make the commitment to change experience the most trouble with installing EI programs. With commitment being the kingpin to launching a successful program, small and mid-size companies may have the advantage.

 *E*mployee involvement activities are supported by establishing long-term goals and clear objectives and having one person responsible for advancing the program.

Competitive pressures are making companies more interested in gains relating to productivity, quality, and employee motivation. Morale is also a key concern of management. These all directly affect the bottom line of the organization and are the reasons so many companies are embracing some type of employee involvement program.

Improving Productivity

Boosting productivity is the cheapest way to raise profits and the key to flexibility in these fast-changing times. Although American companies generally restructured their operations earlier than their international counterparts, only the best among them have a significant edge. Many of the companies leading the recovery with productivity gains can attribute their improvement to predictable upticks in cyclical industries. Low productivity and poor quality continue to challenge many organizations.

Fortunately, many recent advancements in human resource management address the productivity challenge. EI programs emphasize participation and teamwork, TQM programs require continuous quality improvement, and new empowerment and incentive programs encourage worker motivation. Exhibit 5–9 lists some of the newer made-in-America management ideas, including team management, total quality management, broadbanding, worker empowerment, and skill-based pay. Some companies are going beyond quality to pursue long-term productivity gains by committing their resources to employee learning (discussed later in the "Training and Development" section).

According to a study conducted by the Electric Power Research Institute, total quality management, which calls on employee teams to devise their own ways of improving their own productivity, is the most popular approach with large companies. The study also revealed that employee and customer satisfaction with other short-lived management approaches is very low.

Although evidence is building against some of the more popular approaches, they each can succeed in certain situations. And enough companies are succeeding to prompt others to give them a try. It's clear, however, that there are no management panaceas. Trial and error will accompany most new systems, with the result likely being a unique version that works for the organization. Traditional practices will continue giving way to new ones.

Any new program should be introduced slowly. In an incremental approach, small groups or departments are trained and rewarded after reaching their goals. This disarms employee apprehension and fosters worker support. The program can also be evaluated for its value to the organization and support of the vision (Exhibit 5–5).

Recruitment. Employees play a big part in affecting customer satisfaction. Workers must be competent in many areas to be effective in meeting or exceeding customer expectations; they must be knowledgeable, reliable, courteous, responsive, and so forth. The value of frontline employees has been the subject of much research, policy debate, and business discussion.[11] But even without this attention, we all recognize the importance of working with competent colleagues and having quality personnel serve us at banks, post offices, restaurants, and hospitals.

EXHIBIT 5-9
New Ideas in Management

Team building—Efforts made to foster teamwork and improve communication within organizations.

Total quality management—Individuals and teams given responsibility for improving product and service quality.

Broadbanding—Multiple salary grades reduced for greater worker flexibility.

Reengineering—The work process reorganized to more effectively create products and services for customers.

Employee/team empowerment—Power and authority delegated to subordinates.

Skill-based pay—Employees' pay increases based on their improved competencies.

Employee involvement—Employees participate in planning how firm operates.

Partnering—Various programs, such as profit sharing, give employees a stake in the company.

Career pathing—Employees receive training and development for advancement purposes.

Managing diversity—Diversity integrated into the workplace: race, disability, sexual orientation, gender, age, culture, and ethnicity.

Pay for performance—Compensation based on the value added by employees to products and services.

Job enrichment—Depth and challenge of job increased for greater worker motivation.

The following guidelines can help you to "hire smart," that is, to establish a workforce capable of delivering world-class customer satisfaction:

1. Hire a "business partner". Put a similar amount of resources into hiring employees as you would if you were hiring a partner. This means using whatever it takes to discover employees who have the right mix of characteristics that will enhance your organization's vision. Commit the time and effort. According to Robert Foley, Guest Quarter's senior vice president for human resources, they see it as a 50-50 relationship: "We pay them fairly and give them a good benefit plan and their commitment to us is that they will be customer oriented."[12]

Many firms call employees *associates*—don't, unless their responsibilities, authority, and opportunities back it up.

2. Test the culture fit. Identify the values that stem from your company vision and the culture that results. Evaluate employees on their fit with this culture, based on their shared values and their contribution to furthering the vision. Swissair assesses how candidates fit with its company culture that requires putting the passenger first, being patient, and not being too authoritarian.[13] Nordstrom emphasizes personal chemistry and an upbeat attitude more than experience or technical knowledge for their salesclerks.

3. Use employee input. By allowing employees to attend or even to conduct interviews, you can obtain their important perspective of a candidate's ability to fit in. Nordstrom relies on employees to sniff out the right personalities for the job. This also sends a clear message to prospective candidates about how management values employee opinion. The Union Square Cafe in New York requires candidates to go through five interviews with five different staff members who then make recommendations to management. At Chi-Chi's, a "star server" sometimes conducts a second interview with a job applicant, a practice that significantly helps establish teamwork once the candidate is hired.

Employees observing or conducting interviews should consider:

- How will the candidate do (image, efficiency, effectiveness) in front of the customer (assuming they were given appropriate training)?
- How will the candidate get along with other employees?
- Will he or she be a team player?
- Does the person really want to work here?
- Is the person capable or skilled enough for the job applied for?
- Will he or she help the organization grow in the direction it wants to go? How?
- Will the person be able to represent this organization's philosophy and approach to customer satisfaction?
- What in the person's background proves that he or she is likely to succeed at this job?

4. Find "customer champions." What is the candidate's philosophy of service? Many outstanding service companies like McDonald's or Embassy Suites have designated sets of abilities and personality traits that help in satisfying customers. They probe candidates for those characteristics with psychological tests and behavioral interviews. These procedures ask how the candidates have acted or would act in various situations.

Simulations based on procedures used in the Second World War to pick spies were first applied by AT&T in 1966. The company showed that these tests revealed considerable accuracy in predicting candidates' accomplishments up to eight years after hiring. At Tuma's restaurant in Mt. Pleasant, Michigan, management will place a dirty napkin on the floor and observe candidates as they walk across the room. Any candidate who doesn't stop and pick it up is disqualified.

In one popular type of simulation exercise, candidates are presented with common problems in their hypothetical in-baskets. This can give valuable insight into a candidate's management style, including her or his ability to delegate, make appropriate decisions, deal with others, and maintain a customer perspective. A software program called "InnBasket," produced by the Educational Institute in East Lansing, Michigan [(800) 344-4381)], has users play the part of a hotel manager with limited time to handle 18 problems. In another simulation exercise, the person is informed that he or she has been promoted and will have to leave town for an important meeting. The candidate is given one hour to deal with memos, letters, reports, telephone messages, and other materials left by the previous employee.

You can also create your own simulation by asking candidates to role-play a situation. Sample scenarios for a frontline sales or customer service candidate could include:[14]

- Simple sales call—Persuade caller to purchase more than he or she initially asked for and complete forms summarizing the sale.
- Difficult customer—Respond to caller who is uncooperative and eventually abusive.
- Established customer—Resolve a dispute over a late payment. The customer moved and received the bill late, resulting in a late-payment fee. Candidate must write a memo to the supervisor about the incident.

Other approaches to evaluate a candidate's service aptitude include exams, work sampling, and a guest-relations video test.[15]

 *R*eview the selection process in your company for its ability to detect customer-oriented candidates. Even positions having no external client contact will have internal customer relationships.

Companies can gain a strong competitive advantage through hiring and training better people than their competitors do. Singapore Airlines flight attendants are known for their beauty and poise; McDonald's employees are courteous; IBM employees are professional and knowledgeable; Disney workers (cast members) are friendly and upbeat. Certain companies such as Merck and Hewlett-Packard, set their sales forces apart from the competition with exceptional training programs. Williams-Sonoma and Wal-Mart have become known for their greeters who welcome shoppers, offer them advice on where to find merchandise, and mark items brought back for returns or exchanges.

But there are many more examples of poor hiring practices. Banks, airlines, hotels, insurance companies, investment firms, consumer products companies, and countless other industries are burdened with high employee turnover. For example, the food service industry, the largest single employer in the United States, is plagued with a nearly 300 percent annual employee turnover rate. That means that a newly hired employee will last an average of only four months. In 1990 the costs of hiring this new employee (advertising, recruiting, management and clerical time, interviewing, training, and so on) was about $2,000 in direct costs and an additional $1,400 in indirect costs (the drain on morale and the loss of public goodwill). The cost of turnover at the managerial level is estimated to be about $17,000 to $20,000 per employee.[16] Turnover is a multifaceted disaster of monumental proportions.

Hiring the right people is difficult. It is also the first step to reducing turnover. Career development, benefit plans, and other strategies can help to keep employees, but without picking the right people from the start, no personnel program can help to satisfy the needs of your customers.

Ritz-Carlton Hotels uses an effective selection process to find "ladies and gentlemen" to staff its hotels. Called *character trait recruiting*, the system is designed to evaluate a candidate for one of the company's 120 job positions. The approach's high level of correct predictions has reduced turnover considerably since its introduction.

An employee's initial experience can significantly affect her or his future performance and help to reduce turnover. The employee orientation should leave a long and lasting impression. As one researcher put it: "The employee who feels welcome and important will make the customer feel welcome and important. Most leading service corporations treat their employees' first day on the job as a cause for a two-way celebration."[17] At Triad Systems, a California-based computer company, president and chief executive officer James Porter finds time to invite new hires over to his home for dinner. Other senior executives do the same.[18]

Establish and consistently follow an orientation program that does much more than merely explain the mechanics of the job. Explain the company's goals, philosophy, and culture to all applicants. For new employees, review this information or provide additional details.[19] Utilize the vision statement (refer to Exhibit 5–5) and demonstrate through examples that it has real meaning. Showing that management values employees and their peers can have a lasting effect on new hires. This type of nonmonetary treatment of workers fosters employee loyalty.

Uncommitted employers. Companies typically don't demonstrate loyalty to their workers, and employees recognize this. Firms accept this situation and even anticipate it. General Motors and American Express require executives to include a "no compete" clause in their contract, which prohibits them from defecting to a competitor for three years after they leave the company. American Express also requires a nonsolicitation agreement to prevent executives from consulting with competitors if they leave the company. Contracts with Compaq Computers and other high-tech firms use "bad boy" clauses to prevent managers from taking others with them if they quit (talent raids). But coercing employee allegiance through legalities is, at best, a short-term fix. Workers are forging a change in their definition of worker loyalty: they are asking if their company is loyal to *them*.

Career pathing is growing in popularity, not only as an effective recruiting and development tool, but because employees will not stay without long-term opportunities. Workers are looking for increased financial and job security. The Food Waiter Servers Association, for example, pushes for career opportunities for its members. This national organization strives to elevate the standards and status of the 1.8 million food servers in the United States. The group provides health insurance, job contacts, a newsletter offering tips on how to improve skills, reviews of service-related books, and a who's who listing of American waiters.[20]

Employee assistance programs (EAPs). Another effective way management can address employees' personal concerns is through work-life support programs, also known as employee assistance programs (EAPs) or family life, dependent care, and child care programs. These programs are expanding rapidly because they have been shown to increase employee satisfaction.

The quality of the company's health care package influences employee satisfaction. Marriott changed the name of its program to "work-life" to attract a wider range of employees. More than including psychological counseling and expanded dental and eye care coverage, companies are slowly developing programs to accommodate the lifestyle needs of single mothers, childless couples, and other employees without families. Despite new regulations such as the federal family-leave law, training managers to be more family friendly is the top priority of many new work-family programs.

Companies are using new approaches to address employees' child care problems. Instead of spending huge amounts of money to construct their own centers, employers are customizing child care solutions for individual cases. Besides providing low cost space within current facilities, some companies offer child care subsidies, advisory committees, seminar programs, and resource libraries. Some businesses, however, have found that there is not enough demand for an organized program because relatives and friends already provide the essential service. Such companies can solve child care problems that do arise by matching providers with a family's unique needs.

EAPs are growing in popularity with employees and employers. Many of these programs offer a full range of psychological services such as individual, couple, and family counseling, burnout prevention, stress reduction, drug and alcohol dependency treatment, and crisis intervention. For workers, these private, professional counseling services are a prized benefit that not only save them money but also encourage them to seek assistance with their personal problems. For employers, they are new tools for maintaining and improving customer service.

Employers adopt EAPs because they realize that employee attendance and stability affects customer satisfaction. A quality EAP program will reduce the days that employees miss and will improve the continuity of service. For example, business customers want to see familiar faces when they travel and appreciate being acknowledged by name. The more stable a workforce, the more like home a hotel can become.

As awareness of a program increases, people feel more comfortable utilizing these services. Although only several of the large hotel chains (Four Seasons, Sheraton, Westin, and Marriott) have added EAPs to their benefit packages, all major and most smaller hotel chains will make EAP services available by the year 2000.[21] Ninety percent of Fortune 500 companies already offer EAPs.

No-fault layoffs. The story is told of a company that set off its fire alarms in order to assemble all employees in the parking lot outside, where it announced a layoff. Only those still having jobs were allowed to reenter the building; those laid off had their personal possessions collected by their supervisors and carried out to them in the parking lot.[22]

People will go to great lengths to avoid the discomforts associated with terminating an employee. But for more substantial reasons, firms are finding creative ways to reduce their labor costs and still keep their employees working. Some of these approaches to reduce layoffs include lending surplus employees to other employers, work sharing, and retraining employees for other positions in the firm.

Motivating dissatisfied workers. Job enrichment tries to deal with unsatisfied workers by increasing the depth of a job with more autonomy and responsibility. Known as *vertical job loading*, the principle is that as work becomes more challenging, the employee's motivation and enthusiasm also increase. But it's not for everybody. Persons with high growth needs will be more satisfied in expanded and challenging jobs than those with low growth needs. Employees are motivated by different things. These may include recognition, increased responsibility, potential for advancement, personal encouragement, or cash incentives.

Satisfying customers on behalf of the organization can be more motivating than simply working to make more money for your employer. An organization's profits have no intrinsic or humanistic value. But performing for the benefit of customers is an entirely different matter. Satisfying customers is a goal steeped in positive humanistic value.[23]

The information obtained through customer, employee, management, and competitive inputs will call for constant change. Implementation is a continuous process and employee motivation is essential for any lasting improvements. Employee enthusiasm is required simply to maintain current levels of customer satisfaction.

Empowerment. A general manager of a large hotel in San Francisco explains the meaning of empowerment:

We had an Australian group here—five of them. They went into the bar and asked for Foster's Lager, which we don't carry. They were very disappointed. The bartender said, "Why don't you have this instead, and we'll see what we can do in the future." They said, "O.K., but we'd like you to know we're going to be here five days." By the time they ordered the second drink, the bartender had a case of Foster's Lager in the bar's cooler. She'd gone across the street and bought it with her own money. That's what this is all about—the customer comes first. The bartender never questioned whether she'd be reimbursed; of course she was, and she'd do it again.

Empowerment is based on trust between superior and subordinate because it gives additional power and authority to employees.

Service Wars

At the Hyatt Regency, Chicago, every employee carries a card that says, "Empowerment: I am free to take care of the guest, and management will support me."

At Ritz-Carlton Hotels, employees are empowered "to move heaven and earth" to satisfy guests. They may spend up to $2,000 per guest, and be reimbursed, to accomplish this.

Encouraging Professional and Personal Development

Training and Development. Commitment to corporate training and development is making a comeback from the low level it was at during the early 1980s. Many companies, recognizing that knowledge is becoming antiquated at a faster rate, are using formal classroom training, apprenticeship programs, or other forms of innovative pedagogy to develop employees. Although there are few reliable yardsticks to measure the effectiveness of employee learning, many businesses such as General Electric, U.S. Robotics, W.H. Brady, and Texas Instruments are taking the risk and expanding their investments in it.

Motorola is a leader in this knowledge-based strategy. Having one of the finest reputations for quality in the United States, Motorola fears that quality is not enough; it believes that responsiveness, adaptability, and creativity will be the decisive competencies by the turn of the century. They currently give employees at least 40 hours of education per year and spend 4.6 percent of payroll expenses on training.

Motorola's programs stand out for their ability to tie business objectives to classroom topics. For example, they developed a course dedicated exclusively to decreasing product development time. They teach statistical process control to employees on the shop floor to reduce error rates and improve quality. They also require this course for international suppliers that have trouble meeting quality specifications. Through its Motorola University, the company is even bringing this targeted learning approach to public schools. Students in the pilot program are trained in such areas as communication, problem solving, and teamwork skills and are evaluated according to the jargon of the quality movement: *change needed, achieved standard, and exceeds standard.*[24]

Other current approaches in organizational training focus on imparting sensitivity and greater understanding to employees. One approach, called *empathy training*, includes a variety of cross-training and experiential techniques. For example, schools use it to teach understanding of people with disabilities. Students try to get around in wheelchairs, eat blindfolded, and so forth.

Empathy training is useful to organizations in two ways. Through its first dimension, cross-training, employees learn to perform the functions of the personnel in other areas of their organization. This can be very effective in improving relationships between internal customers. Once trained, employees perform these new duties for a short period of time, from one to three months. The purpose is to foster understanding among employees of different departments by giving them the chance to empathize with their peers. The results are better communication, reduced antagonism, and sometimes the development of better procedures.

The other dimension of empathy training, experiential learning, helps employees identify with the customer. Employees are directed to go through the entire customer experience to understand how their attitudes and behavior can affect their clients' satisfaction. Employees not only better understand how to serve their customers, they also see how their own work affects the entire customer experience.

Teamwork. Teams are the building blocks of world-class organizations. Supervisory roles are limited by making groups manage themselves. They are given a clear purpose and are held accountable for measurable performance goals.

Teams direct most employee activities at Ritz-Carlton Hotels. At each level of the company—from corporate leaders to managers and employ-

EXHIBIT 5–10
Guidelines for Creating Teams

- Have a purpose. What is the reason for forming teams? Set goals and time limits.
- Select members carefully. Who should participate? Should membership change?
- Set parameters. What issues will they deal with. How much authority will they have? What problems could they cause?
- Measure team output. How will this be measured? Give it a chance; but if it doesn't work, scrap the whole thing and don't blame the team members.

---

ees—teams are responsible for setting objectives and devising action plans. Group problem solving is practiced within hotel departments (functional), between hotel departments (cross-functional), and less frequently, among Ritz-Carlton Hotels (national, cross-functional).

The company believes this approach has led to important benefits. These include proactive thinking beyond day-to-day operations, increased lateral communication among the diverse functions that make up each hotel, and an integrated approach to problem solving.[25]

From improving interdepartmental communication and coordination to allying with customers in group efforts to solve their problems, teams are becoming commonplace approaches to achieving organizational objectives. Exhibit 5–10 presents guidelines for creating teams.

Alternative Schedules. Two types of alternative schedules are being incorporated into the workplace: compressed workweeks and flextime. Compressed workweeks (e.g., 10 hours per day for four days, 12 hours per day for three days, and so on, instead of traditional 8-hour days) reduce employer costs of overtime, overhead, and personal leave time. They also allow spouses to share household responsibilities, attend school, or pursue other activities of their choosing.[26]

Flextime which is popular in Europe, permits employees to arrange their work hours to suit their personal needs. Typically, employees pick their own starting and ending times around a core period of about four hours in the middle of the day. Additional employee responsibility is often necessary to coordinate schedules with other employees.

Employee Compensation. Compensation in most companies is based on a simple idea: people are paid for their time. The reason for this

EXHIBIT 5–11
Keys to Incentive Pay Systems

1. Include all employees in the plan to generate companywide cooperation and support.
2. Develop objectives that reflect the company's critical performance areas.
3. Tie the incentive program to the company's bottom line so that payments won't be made unless the company is profitable.
4. Establish a regular form of communication with employees.
5. Keep payments separate from base wages for greater visibility.
6. Listen to employees for modifications and methods of bringing about effective changes.
7. Review the program regularly for appropriate challenges and incentives.

is obvious. Workers are paid a wage or salary because the value of their work is not easily quantified and isn't comparable. It's much easier to document length of time than real value to the organization. What, for example, is the real value of a doorman's greeting or a chef's preparation of a salad? Neither has any value by itself. Only the entire hotel experience or the complete meal has value to the company. Companies have no choice but to measure workers on the efficiency with which they perform narrowly defined tasks.[27] Instead of simply measuring time, however, some companies measure performance on the basis of the value created. They do so by implementing incentive pay systems. Exhibit 5–11 presents keys to such pay systems.

By figuring out how much employees actually contribute to products and services, companies can pay them according to their value-added contributions. Although in most cases this is very difficult to accomplish, many companies are incorporating this pay-for-performance approach as part of their compensation to employees.

How can this be done? One approach used by IBM Credit measures not how many pieces of paper an employee handles, but the profitability of the final deal and the quality of work, as reflected in customer satisfaction surveys. This approach emphasizes rewards and downplays progressive wage and salary increases.

Confident with the success of this approach, IBM dramatically changed the way they pay their salespeople. Under the new plan, 60 percent of a salesperson's income will be determined by the profitability of an order.

Few companies have tied so much pay to profits. To protect against over-zealous employees who might otherwise push fast-turnover, high-margin products instead of focusing on real customer needs, IBM ties the remaining 40 percent of salespersons' income to customer satisfaction.

Clients are surveyed to evaluate how pleased they were with the sales team and if the representatives helped them achieve their business objectives. This high-percentage payback for customer satisfaction is among the most aggressive employed by large companies.

Service Wars
American Express Publishing's Database Media Group announced that all magazine jobs will be redefined in terms of customer satisfaction rather than, for example, meeting quotas or ad sales.

Any incentive pay system must be fair in the eyes of employees to avoid recrimination and jealousy. The system should be based on objective evaluation and distributed equitably.

Marriott's Fairfield Inn uses a highly innovative approach that has been well accepted by employees. This simple PC-driven checkout game called *Scorecard* requires about 15 seconds to play and encourages guests to provide feedback on the cleanliness of their room, the level of hospitality at check-in and checkout, and the overall value of their experience. But the exceptional part of this automated comment card is that responses are keyed to the times they were filled out and provide daily customer feedback by employees. Receptionists and housekeepers (the only two levels of employees) can earn up to 10 percent of their compensation through guest evaluations. These are frontline employees earning money from customer satisfaction. Managers can earn up to 20 percent of their compensation directly from the Scorecard ratings.

Compensation systems should promote the following messages to employees:

- Customers pay our salaries.
- We are rewarded for doing a better job.
- We are encouraged to improve our job skills.
- Our income is maximized through constant improvement of customer satisfaction.

Another innovative way to link compensation with customer satisfaction is through vendors. This type of partnering links customer surveys with incentives to get suppliers motivated to satisfy your customers. By tying a considerable amount of their contract to your customer evaluations, suppliers become a partner by assuming some of your customer responsibility. This share-the-risk approach is likely to become a key operating strategy for years to come.[28]

By sharing the risk with employees and suppliers, companies encourage individual contributions to customer satisfaction. When these contributions are combined, additional value is created. The added value of combining individual outputs benefits shareholders, customers, the organization, employees, and suppliers. This approach motivates individuals and groups to produce on behalf of all the firm's constituencies. For employees or suppliers, the emphasis is shifted to maximizing customer satisfaction instead of focusing on personal goals or making more widgets.

 *M*easure employee and supplier performance by their contribution to customer satisfaction. Pay them according to how effectively they achieve this goal.

There are many ways to encourage employees to work hard at pleasing customers. For example, with less than 1,500 employees, Triad Corporation spends over $40,000 and gives out more than 700 awards per year to deserving employees. They believe that recognition is the key ingredient to building a positive and productive culture.

Successful reward systems include:

- Profit sharing.
- Flexible, cafeteria-style ("pick what looks best") benefits.
- Employee stock ownership plans.
- Nonmonetary recognition awards for performance.
- Gainsharing.
- Individual incentives.[29]

Profit sharing and employee stock ownership programs, used by companies for over 10 years, have proven successful. But in the past five years an unprecedented number of companies initiated some type of ownership program; and these companies, since beginning these programs, have been more profitable than those without such incentives. Gainsharing, although only several years old, is increasing in popularity. Work group and team incentives, also relatively new, are effective pay-for-performance approaches. Skill-based pay systems (pay based on the number of skills an employee possesses even if they don't directly relate to the specific job being performed at the time) and flexible benefits have also been quite successful, partly because certain consulting firms will provide all of the necessary details and assist with their implementation.[30]

The objective of all of these approaches—motivating employees to become more productive—needs to be regularly evaluated and tied in with longer-term employer and employee objectives. Unfortunately, the most commonly used evaluation practices do not accomplish this effectively.

The traditional reward process, centering on performance appraisal, is still used as the primary tool to manage employee productivity. This is an annual, or semiannual ritual of formally critiquing employees on their job performance. Employees typically become defensive and resentful, and their performance tends to decline after the meeting.[31]

 The goal of a performance appraisal should be to improve future performance. This includes talking about compensation.

By focusing on customer-oriented goals with practical suggestions, the performance appraisal meeting should be treated as a productivity session. The task of integrating customer-based objectives into employees' job skills and performance areas is easier when they are tied to compensation objectives (see Exhibit 5–11). Employees' compensation objectives should be tied to meeting customer satisfaction objectives. Performance/ compensation reviews should focus on:

- Contributions to the customer process. Justify compensation in terms of value created for the customer.
- Contributions to customer satisfaction. As Frank Perdue says, "measure quality, service, and reliability, not birds per man-hour."[32]

Pay must appropriately correspond to the employee's contribution. Pay your employees what they're worth. The following examples are illustrative: Nearly a hundred years ago Henry Ford recognized that paying his employees high wages allowed them to buy the cars they made. Today, autoworkers at Daimler-Benz can often afford to drive the Mercedes they make. In Philadelphia, Fidelity Bank gave 58 percent raises to 100 of their customer service representatives and authorized them to resolve problems involving up to $1,000. Customer satisfaction soared. McDonald's Japan offers any employee completing seven years of employment a free franchise license to run their own branch store.

A long-term evaluation of employee productivity should take place in a separate development meeting. In such a meeting, employees focus more on career development than on what they are worth. The emphasis in these meetings should be on:

1. Their current fit within the organization, especially regarding how well their ability matches their current job and supports customer-based goals.

2. Their alternatives for progressing.

3. Plans to improve their abilities, that is, what they need to learn and ways to accomplish this goal.

Critical feedback can be obtained from employees about what is needed to improve customer satisfaction. This can be encouraged in this limited focus meeting without the distraction of compensation issues.

However, most companies either combine these issues or confuse them. They should be dealt with separately, focusing on job skills and career growth and encouraging a "How can I improve?" attitude.[33]

The goal of a development or career review should be to assess the ability and professional growth of an employee. This does not include talking about compensation.

Broadbanding.   For many companies, broadbanding is the hottest thing in compensation.[34] In this approach, companies reduce their number of salary levels and lump their employees into salary bands. Workers are paid different amounts (within their band) according to a larger number of measurable accomplishments. With this type of variable pay, workers can be moved around more and individual skills can be compensated. Firms are increasingly learning how to exploit these advantages, and many others have plans to implement such systems.

The Australian government encourages business to adopt broadbanding to better respond to technical and structural changes. In the Australian proposal, companies would be able to compensate individuals for a greater range of work activities, such as for education and training efforts as well as for more traditional gains in productivity.

Johnson & Johnson was a pioneer of broadbanding. But after a year they scrapped the experiment when 6,000 employees complained that they didn't like not having a clear path upward. Others were unhappy about being clumped in a salary band with people who used to be their subordinates. They have now adopted a system at the other end of the spectrum, measuring pay levels against 300 other jobs in the marketplace.[35] Broadbanding is not for everyone.

Service Wars
The First National Bank of Chicago revised teller managers' job descriptions by making them responsible for the front side of the teller counter (managing the lines and ensuring quick transactions) in addition to their traditional duties (e.g., servicing customer accounts, balancing, and so on).[36]

Managing Diversity. By the year 2000, 85 percent of all new entrants into the labor force will be women, minorities, and immigrants. To better understand these employees and meet the special customer needs that stem from race, disability, sexual orientation, gender, age, culture, or ethnicity, companies are starting to offer instruction on workplace diversity.

These unconventional training programs go beyond classroom seminars that simply mix employees together or programs that only put money into troubled community areas. In this new approach, employees at all levels often give considerable time and commitment to a wide range of community needs. These programs give employees firsthand knowledge of the people and problems that make up and surround their businesses. This new understanding results in better service to a wider clientele and generates substantial goodwill and word-of-mouth promotion for the company. It also helps employees grow personally—they feel good about what they're doing—which enhances worker loyalty.

One exemplary program, sponsored annually by UPS, assigns 40 middle and upper-level supervisors to month long community internships. The thought is that living and working in poor communities will help managers better understand employees and customers from diverse backgrounds. However, the program is still regarded with some apprehension. Initially, internships were offered only to workers who had been caught uttering racial slurs or who had a bad record working with minorities. Although the program is receiving continued participation and overall turnover is extremely low (2 percent), the results are hard to measure. To promote employees' involvement and increase the overall effectiveness of such programs, companies should include workers' input into the design and management of them.

Diversity education and other nontraditional approaches to training, offered by such companies as Xerox and Wells Fargo, provide paid leaves to employees who volunteer at nonprofit agencies. At Wells Fargo Bank, more than 200 employees have devoted up to six months for activities such as refurbishing houses in poor neighborhoods and delivering medicine in South America. Smaller companies can also participate. The Glennon Company, an 80-person ad agency, gives employees one day off each month for volunteer work.

 *E*ncourage employees to tackle social issues. Consider offering them a social service leave. Benefits include enhanced community relations, better service to a wider clientele, and improved employee attitudes.

Loews Hotels recognizes the mutual benefits obtained from demonstrating a strong sense of social responsibility through its "Good Neighbor Policy." By focusing on several areas of concern ranging from protecting the environment to aiding the homeless, this outreach program supports the communities where Loews owns and manages its hotels. Under the policy, each hotel is responsible for the following activities:

- Donating excess food from the hotel to local food banks.
- Supporting local literacy programs by providing space for the classes to be held and volunteer instructors from the hotel.
- Recycling all office paper and newspapers and purchasing recycled products, whenever possible.
- Donating used goods, such as furniture, to local organizations.

- Encouraging volunteer activities for hotel employees.
- Implementing energy-saving equipment in new hotels and in existing properties as they are renovated.

Other opportunities for improving service to wider clientele stem from the Americans with Disabilities Act (ADA). This legislation concerns the hiring and serving of disabled persons and is fully enforceable in 1996. The law entitles persons with disabilities to the same rights and services as other Americans. Title III instructs businesses to provide access for disabled people to their facilities and services. Businesses may not discriminate against nor deny service to disabled persons. For example, the law prevents businesses from requiring disabled persons to use a designated seat, imposing a special charge because of the person's disability, or requiring that a person with a disability be accompanied by an attendant. Certainly discriminatory policies have, in the past, decreased the business coming from this sizable market segment. (Companies that see the ADA as an opportunity rather than a constraint can reverse the dissatisfaction and discrimination created and gain a competitive advantage.)

Hiring of disabled persons opens up a large pool of skilled workers. Service companies such as McDonalds, Kentucky Fried Chicken, and Marriott Corporation, for example, are increasingly employing people who have mental retardation.

 *F*ollow and improve upon the ADA regulations for accommodating disabled persons. The opportunity of market expansion makes it cost effective and worthwhile.

Many companies are going beyond the letter of the law. To simply comply, for example, hotels must have telecommunications devices for the deaf (TTDs), closed-captioned decoders, emergency warning systems (bed vibrators, strobe lights, audio alarms) or other necessary equipment (braille materials, phone amplifiers). They must provide accessible bathrooms for disabled guests.

Embassy Suites provides all this and more. It created a disability etiquette training program that is the standard for the chain. The company realizes that there is a large market of disabled persons who have the money to travel and will go out of their way to patronize businesses that make their travel experiences easier.[37]

WORLD-CLASS SOLUTIONS

We have focused on those approaches to employee management that affect the customer and contribute to the redesign process. There is no one magic solution for all the employee problems affecting customer satisfaction. Companies and their employees need to be evaluated on their unique characteristics. What works best for one company or situation may not work for others and may change over time. Employee programs may offer only short-lived advantages and often need adjustment just as customer strategies need to be examined and redesigned.

So how do you keep employees loyal, productive, and growing? Support and encourage these characteristics through the low-cost programs and innovative management approaches discussed in this chapter. Ongoing training and development, realistic career opportunities, incentive and reward structures, and work-life programs will be the crucial areas into the year 2000. Choose those employee programs that directly support your customer service cycles. Turn personnel problems into advantages by launching programs that reward employees for ensuring customer satisfaction.

There are no shortcuts to deliver organizational performance without combining planning tools with effective human resource management. But you can create new ways of handling your basic products and services. Redesign your customer processes. Use appropriate employee programs to support these changes. Give production and quality responsibilities to employees. Remove internal barriers that restrict employees from doing their jobs. And tie the performance of all employees and suppliers to their contribution to customer satisfaction. Organizations and employees will both profit if workers are provided the resources, opportunity, and incentives to excel.

SUMMARY

- Processes are related tasks that provide a product or service to customers. Organize improvement efforts around these customer-driven processes (the service side of the customer service cycle), not around departments such as sales or production.

- Using customer, employee, and competitor information, remove barriers to satisfaction by redesigning existing processes.
- Employees treat customers similar to the way they, as employees, are treated by management.
- Selecting the right employee program can add considerable strength to the design and delivery of your customer processes.
- Creating a passionate and motivated workforce starts with a vision for the organization. Visions should be simple, communicated at every opportunity, and personally conveyed by top management. Create a human resources vision statement embodying the ideal spirit of your organization.
- Just as products and services may be tailored to individual customer needs, a company's personnel issues can be more effectively addressed through customized programs and strategies.
- Eliminate unnecessary levels of management, create worker teams, and give production and quality responsibilities to employees.
- Employee involvement activities are supported by establishing long-term goals and clear objectives and having one person responsible for advancing the program.
- Review the selection process in your company for its ability to detect customer-oriented candidates. Even positions having no external client contact will have internal customer relationships.
- Measure employee and supplier performance by their contribution to customer satisfaction. Pay them according to how effectively they achieve this goal.
- The goal of a performance appraisal should be to improve future performance. This includes talking about compensation.
- The goal of a development or career review should be to assess the ability and professional growth of an employee. This does not include talking about compensation.
- Encourage employees to tackle social issues. Consider offering them a social service leave. Benefits include enhanced community relations, better service to a wider clientele, and improved employee attitudes.
- Follow and improve upon the ADA regulations for accommodating disabled persons. The opportunity for market expansion makes it cost effective and worthwhile.

NOTES

1. Michael Hammer and James Champy, *Reengineering the Corporation: A Manifesto for Business Revolution* (New York: Harper Business, 1993), p. 117.

2. John A. Byrne, "Reengineering: Beyond the Buzzword," *Business Week*, May 24, 1993, p. 12.

3. Hammer and Champy, *Reengineering the Corporation*, pp. 117–39.

4. Jonathan Dahl, "Tracking Travel," *The Wall Street Journal*, May 28, 1993, p. B1.

5. Robert E. Kelley, "Poorly Served Employees Serve Customers Just as Poorly," *The Wall Street Journal*, October 12, 1987, p. 20.

6. This introduction is based on a conversation with Horst Schulze, president of Ritz-Carlton Hotels, August 20, 1993.

7. Based on a telephone conversation with Daryl Hartley-Leonard, president of Hyatt Hotel Corporation, July 4, 1993.

8. Based on a discussion with Jonathan Tisch, president and chief executive officer of Loews Hotels, August 25, 1993.

9. Charles Solomon, "The Loyalty Factor" *Personnel Journal*, September 1992, p. 52.

10. Most of this section is based on the results of a study conducted by the Center for Effective Management and reported in Edward E. Lawler, Susan A. Mohrman, and Gerald E. Ledford, Jr., *Employee Involvement and Total Quality Management: Practices and Results in Fortune 1000 Companies* (San Francisco: Jossey-Bass, 1992).

11. L. L. Berry, A Parasuraman, and V.A. Zeithaml, "The Service Quality Puzzle," *Business Horizons*, September–October 1988, pp. 35–43.

12. William H. Davidow and Bro Uttal, *Total Customer Service* (New York: Harper & Row, 1989), p. 123.

13. Milind M. Lele with Jagdish N. Sheth, *The Customer Is Key* (New York: John Wiley and Sons, 1987), p. 252.

14. Benjamin Schneider and Daniel Schneider, "Development of a Personnel Selection System for a Service Job," in Christopher Lovelock, ed., *Managing Services,* (Englewood Cliffs, NJ: Prentice Hall, 1992), p. 348.

15. Jonathan D. Barsky, "Theory S: Total Customer Service," *The Cornell Hotel and Restaurant Administration Quarterly,* May 1990, p. 93.

16. John J. Hogan, "Turnover and What to Do about It," *The Cornell Hotel and Restaurant Administration Quarterly*, February 1992, p. 40.

17. Robert L. Desatnick, "Building the Customer-Oriented Workforce," *Training and Development Journal*, March 1987, pp. 72–73.
18. Michael Ramundo, "Service Awards Build Culture of Success," *HR Magazine*, August 1992, p. 61.
19. Hogan, "Turnover and What to Do About It," p. 45.
20. Christopher Conte, "The Labor Letter," *The Wall Street Journal*, February 9, 1993, p. 1.
21. Leslee Jaquette, "Delta Will Help Employees Solve Problems," *Hotel and Motel Management*, October 5, 1992, p. 1.
22. Gordon F. Shea, *Company Loyalty: Earning It, Keeping It*, (New York: American Management Association, Membership Publishing Division, 1987), p. 53.
23. David Altany, "One Step beyond Customer Satisfaction," *Industry Week* 239, no. 17 (September 3, 1990), p. 15.
24. "Motorola: Training for the Millennium," *Business Week*, March 28, 1994, pp. 58–60.
25. From The Ritz-Carlton Hotel Company's Malcolm Baldrige National Quality Award application summary, 1992, p. 7.
26. *4 Days, 40 Hours: Reporting a Revolution in Work and Leisure*, Ed. Rivas Poor (Cambridge, MA: Bursk and Poor, 1970), pp. 1–170.
27. Hammer and Champy, *Reengineering the Corporation*, p. 72.
28. Pamela Sebastian, "Pleasing Hospital Patients Can Pay Off," *Positive Impact*, July 1993, p. 2.
29. Center for Effective Organizations, University of Southern California. Fortune 1,000 companies report these reward systems as very successful.
30. D.E. Bloom and J.T. Trahan, *Flexible Benefits and Employee Choice* (New York: Pergamon Press, 1986), pp. 2–50.
31. J. Stoner and R. Freeman, *Management* (Englewood Cliffs, NJ: Prentice Hall, 1989), p. 350.
32. James C. Schaffer, "Push for Quality Service" *Executive Excellence*, November 1992, p. 3.
33. Julie Lopez, "Management," *The Wall Street Journal*, May 10, 1993, p. B1.
34. According to Kenan Abosch of Hewitt Associates, quoted in Fred R. Bleakley, "The Best Laid Plans," *The Wall Street Journal*, July 6, 1993, p. 1.
35. Fred R. Bleakley, "The Best Laid Plans," *The Wall Street Journal*, July 6, 1993, p. 1.

36. Leonard L. Berry and Linda R. Cooper, "Competing with Time-Saving Service" in *Managing Services* ed. Christopher Lovelock (Englewood Cliffs, NJ: Prentice Hall, 1992), p. 172.

37. Edward Watkins and Grace Wagner, "Coping with the ADA," *Lodging Hospitality*, December 1992, pp. 79–80.

Chapter Six

Retention Marketing
Sustaining Profitability through Customer Loyalty, Complaint Management, and Satisfaction Guarantees

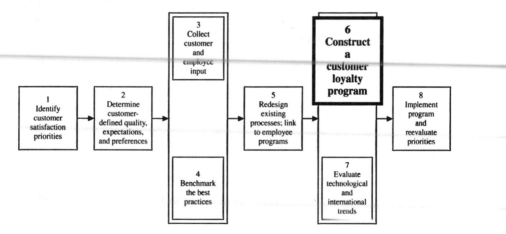

If you would treat every customer like your last or your first, you'd never have to worry about repeat business.

Herb Kelleher, *CEO Southwest Airlines*

Achieving and maintaining customer loyalty is essential for overall profitability. Why?

1. It does wonders for improving cash flow. A loyal customer makes repeat purchases over a long period of time.
2. It costs less to keep a customer than to gain a new one, up to five times less.

3. Repeat customers are more willing to pay higher prices for products and services. They spend more than first-time customers.

4. Current customers bring in new customers. Nothing works better than a personal recommendation.

5. If they're not your customers, their patronage belongs to someone else.

A loyal customer does not buy your toothpaste once or twice, use your travel agency just occasionally, or stay at your hotel sometimes. The loyal customer we're talking about is the person who always uses X toothpaste, swears by the Y Travel Agency, and will stay only at Hotel Z. Once a customer makes a first purchase and then concludes that there is no better choice, a strong and enduring relationship develops. People move up a "loyalty ladder" from trial buyer, to client, to advocate, as shown in Exhibit 6–1.

Every time potential customers consider purchasing a product, they are confronted with barriers to this decision. These can range from the inconvenience of finding the product or not knowing anything about its benefits to larger barriers, such as having had a positive experience with a competing brand. Companies must understand these obstacles to overcome them. The challenge is to anticipate and remove, or at least decrease, these obstructions.

Barriers to buying products and services include:[1]

- *Switching costs*—Price of changing patronage habits. Examples of customer reactions are "I can't leave my barber . . . he knows what I like!" or "I'm almost halfway to Europe in frequent-flier miles! I must keep flying Puddle Jump Airlines." Switching costs include search costs, transaction costs, learning costs, loyal customer discounts, customer habit, emotional cost, and physical and mental effort.

- *Perceived risks*—Unknown component of new purchase. A customer reaction may be: "How do I know if this car will be as reliable as my Honda?" Perceived risks include the financial, social, and psychological risks associated with the purchase of a new product or service.

- *Lack of information*—Information about current market alternatives. "I didn't know The Ritz was offering a 50 percent discount on weekends." Lack of information includes lack of knowledge about a product, competitors, and the general market.

EXHIBIT 6–1
The Customer Loyalty Ladder

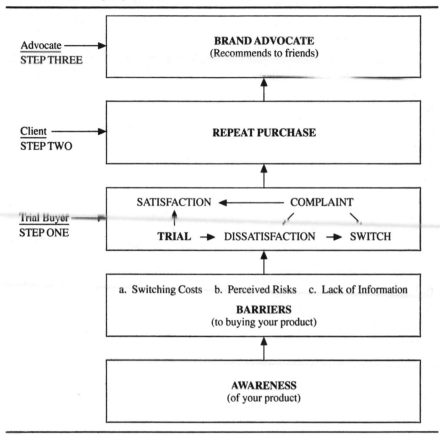

Together these add up to the barriers or forces that can prevent or discourage customers from changing brands. Then again, customers often just feel like a change for the sake of change.

Brand loyalty was a popular research topic in the 1950s and 1960s. Early studies simply proved the existence of brand loyalty and concluded that most consumers are brand loyal.[2] Since then brand loyalty, sometimes called *customer* or *owner loyalty,* has been closely linked to customer satisfaction. Satisfied customers are more likely to repeat and increase their purchase.[3] It is now widely recognized that loyal customers are essential for long-term business success.[4] As a result, repeat patronage is a fundamental marketing objective.

But for all of the importance placed on customer loyalty, relatively few firms dedicate efforts to creating and maintaining repeat business. Many businesses have neglected this potent source of profitability. The purpose of this chapter is to consider various strategies and tactics that companies can use to create more loyal customers, also referred to as *retention* marketing. Although everything a firm does affects customer loyalty, several focused approaches can directly increase repeat business. These include a combination of loyalty programs, effective complaint management, and offering satisfaction guarantees.

LOYALTY PROGRAMS

Stanley Marcus of Neiman-Marcus department stores identifies the importance of keeping customers as the most important lesson he ever learned in retailing. A woman once returned a damaged lace gown she had obviously mistreated. Stanley's father instructed his son to give the woman a full refund and to "do it with a smile." Over the years, that woman spent over $500,000 at Neiman-Marcus.

 *T*he cost of retaining a loyal customer is only one-fifth that of attracting a new one.[5]

Stanley Marcus learned about the long term profit that repeat customers represent and about the costs associated with *keeping* a customer versus *attracting* a new one. He uncovered several critical concepts that are still true today:

- The majority of an average company's business comes from its present satisfied customers.
- It costs a lot more to acquire a new customer than to service an existing one.
- Repeat customers spend more than first time customers, that is, over time their purchase amounts tend to increase.

Despite these compelling facts, many companies focus their efforts on attracting new customers and invest relatively little in services and promotions directed at current customers. Exhibit 6–2 portrays an exception. As reflected in the card, Columbia House knows it is more cost effective to encourage previous customers to repurchase than to attract new customer purchases.

It can be easier to sell to previous customers because they have lower barriers, or less resistance, to repurchasing products; therefore, promotions are likely to be more effective when directed to them. Companies should emphasize the advantages of being a loyal customer in these promotions.

Frequent-Customer Benefits

Customers benefit from their own loyalty. Superior service, improved efficiency, and better overall value are some of the advantages earned by customers making repeated purchases. When you're a familiar face at a restaurant, employees may greet you by name and give you the preferred table. Continued patronage has also taught you when to arrive, where to park, and which items to order or stay away from. A comparable experience is not readily available to others, especially not to a first-time customer. The customer benefits of brand loyalty keep accumulating and, like a good investment, increase in value over time.

But most businesses and their customers don't enjoy this harmonious relationship. In fact, many organizations have no format for recognizing repeat customers. The danger is that without some acknowledgment of customers' repeat business, their products and services soon become indistinguishable from others. Can you tell the difference between brand painkillers, bottled water, paper towels, auto dealers, or similarly priced hotels? Probably not. This is the result of indistinguishable products and services, cost reductions, poor management, excessive staff reduction, employee turnover, and short-term price wars, which have no lasting effect other than making customers price loyal instead of brand loyal. It's no wonder customer loyalty has diminished in the 90s.

Customers need direction and patience to realize the benefits of remaining loyal. Many companies *do* treat loyal customers differently. The Pacific Bell phone company allows "established" customers (those of over one year) an extra 15 days to pay bills and will be flexible in making other payment arrangements with them. This is not an advertised perk.

EXHIBIT 6–2
The Columbia House "Loyalty" Greeting Card

EXHIBIT 6–3
Thrifty Car Rental "Frequent Renter" Program

FREQUENT RENTER

For every 10 rentals receive 2 free days!

Present this card for validation with every rental. When card is complete,
submit this card for TWO FREE DAYS RENTAL OF A FULL SIZE
CAR. Offer not available with any other coupons or certificates and subject
to availability. Card must be filled within 2 years of date of first rental to
receive free offer. This program applies for rentals and redemptions, only in
San Francisco Downtown and Airport offices.

Customer Name *J. Bersky*
Beginning Date *5/25/63*

Thrifty Car Rental

Many companies try to show appreciation and at the same time encourage
brand loyalty through a variety of approaches such as membership clubs,
catalogs, magazines, and, the most common, frequent-user programs.

Frequent-user programs. Frequent-user programs should be
part of a comprehensive relationship marketing effort, discussed later in
this chapter. Although these programs may not, by themselves, build true,
enduring loyalty, they can offer real marketing value and serve as a powerful inducement to return.

 *F*requent-user programs reward faithful customers and provide incentives to encourage repeat business.

In the 1980s, airlines introduced the concept of bonus miles for frequent fliers. This was followed by programs for frequent sleepers (hotels),
frequent shoppers (retailers and credit card companies), frequent drivers
(car rental; see Exhibit 6–3), and even frequent eaters (restaurants). Mail-
order book and record clubs, subscription services, and even ice cream
stores (free cone after buying 12 others) have long understood the value of

EXHIBIT 6–4
Guidelines for Creating a Successful Frequent-User (Loyalty) Program

---

The program should be:
- *Effective*—Emphasize added value rather than discounting. Each "point" earned should make the next point more valuable. Create incentives for customers to continue doing business with you. Give the customers a perception that their "investment" is growing and will be maximized over time.
- *Simple*—New customers must be able to understand the crux of the program within one minute and not be intimidated by the remaining details. Clarify whether points accumulated through corporate or professional membership are redeemable for personal use.
- *Convenient*—Most membership cards should be the size of a standard business card.
- *Memorable*—Keep customers up to date. Promote loyalty programs with member cards, mailings, additional contests, in-store merchandising, and publicity. Newsletters or personalized letters keep interest up and information current.
- *Profitable*—Design a unique system to prevent tampering. Use special stickers, unusual card punches, or an in-house tracking system. Use creative, yet profitable, incentives to maintain customer interest.

---

loyal customers. Now more businesses are catching on and using better-defined programs, avoiding the mistakes of earlier attempts.[6]

The airlines' frequent-flier programs have spread to hotel and restaurant chains. Restaurant chains were attracted by the ability of these programs to encourage customers to visit their other restaurants. Holiday Inn's Priority Club started their frequent-stay program in 1983 (the longest-running such program) to increase chain loyalty. Hotel frequent-stay programs have not produced the intense brand loyalty that the airlines' programs have, partly because travelers base hotel stays on location or service rather than freebies.[7] (Exhibit 6–4) presents guidelines for creating a frequent-user program.

Loyalty programs can get quite elaborate. For example, at a customer's first meal at any restaurant of a Phoenix-based, 10-unit chain, he or she receives a loyalty card with the guest check. Each time the customer visits any one of the restaurants (six different concepts), he or she gets a sticker for the card. After five meals, the customer turns in the card and gets his or her sixth meal free with the purchase of another entrée. The customer then receives a second card. After five more visits to any of the chain's restaurants, the customer can redeem the card for a free dinner, with the purchase of another entrée, and two complimentary desserts or a bottle of wine. Five stickers on a third card earns $50 off the next bill. The customer also gets a Diners Deluxe card, which entitles him or her to 20 percent off any meal purchased within 12 months.[8]

By offering additional benefits such as double stamping on rainy and slow nights, preferred reservations, invitations to wine tastings, theater tickets, selections from a merchandise catalog, or a chance to win a fantasy vacation, a program can keep its allure while not becoming too expensive. Corporate loyalty programs can maintain their professional level by offering such incentives as secretary awards, executive perks, or Christmas luncheons for an entire department. An increased mailing list also offsets the costs of these programs. Even employees can be tied in to the program by offering them incentives to increase customer use of the program.

Despite the complex scoring procedures and costly tracking systems, companies are not shying away from frequent customer programs. They are a value added perk just like trading stamps were in the 60s and 70s. And the participation by so many companies across a variety of products and services make these programs less likely to disappear.

Service Wars
"We'll go as far as we have to earn customer loyalty. Loyal customers shop more often, spend more time in the store, and generally find more merchandise that they're happy with."

Jim Nordstrom, *Nordstrom Inc.*

Credit card companies are also offering their own frequent-buyer programs. American Express offers a nationwide dining program discounting meals 20 percent at participating restaurants. Some cards offer cash rebates, depending on how much the customer buys with the card. This incentive rewards customers for keeping the credit card, using it more often, and making larger purchases. The Sears Discover Card has gained increased acceptance since its debut in 1986, partly due to the allure of a rebate incentive. Other companies that followed this success and created their own rebate cards are General Motors, General Electric, and Ford.

Some frequent-buyer programs have crash-landed because of their complexity. Air Miles, for example, offered free flights for buying consumer goods (*People* magazine subscribers, for example, earned 100 miles) and services (a Hertz weekend car rental paid 25 miles). But consumers found it inconvenient to clip proofs of purchase and mail them in to receive mileage credit. They also had to buy a lot of merchandise to get even small awards. Members had to buy 30,000 pounds of dog food for an airline upgrade!

 *C*reate a frequent customer program—but keep it simple.

Starting a frequent-buyer program can be expensive;[9] so making it last is crucial, both for the customer and the company. As an alternative, companies can use incentives to attract repeat customers without establishing a frequent buyer program. Offering recognition rewards is a low-cost, low-risk alternative that avoids a long-term investment. The high-priced Fairmont Hotels created a President's Club which rewards repeat business with gifts. A Fairmont terrycloth robe is the gift after a third stay. Other options for an informal awards program include an invitation-only plan (e.g., inviting only VIPs to participate) or on-the-spot rewards for some customers.

 *O*ffering customers recognition rewards is a low-cost, low-risk alternative to frequent-buyer programs that avoids a long-term investment.

A magazine, *Inside Flyer,* offers details and tips about frequent-flyer programs. Put out by FlightPlan Inc. of Colorado Springs, Colorado, it costs $33 per year and has 72,000 subscribers. Airlines, hotels, car rental companies, and credit card businesses go to FlightPlan's president, Randy Petersen, to learn the latest about their rivals' programs. Petersen earns about $1 million per year helping companies and individuals purchase miles, transfer free tickets, and read the fine print.

There are many creative approaches companies can use to enhance or go beyond traditional frequent buyer programs. One controversial approach, called "Friends and Families," was introduced with tremendous success by MCI. This long-distance program signed up 10 million people in 22 months, probably the most successful product launch in the history of American business.

In exchange for the names and telephone numbers of frequently called friends and family, customers would receive 20 percent off their future charges to these numbers if these people became new MCI customers. What MCI got was an extremely powerful marketing tool. They were able to approach millions of potential new customers whose friends and family had "recommended" them, and using hard-sell tactics, persuade these people to sign up.

Other innovative approaches to building customer loyalty include:

- Credit card companies offer rebate and warrantee programs.
- New-owner orientation seminars are offered with up-date programs.
- Quality fashion designers offer new styles and colors to match their previous lines.
- Providing special equipment helps prevent customer defections. Federal Express supplies steady customers with tracking software, linked to their headquarters in Memphis.
- Automatic memberships in frequent-buyer clubs are generated by gathering names from receipts. NBO Stores identified big spenders from alteration cards and credit card receipts.
- Warehouse retailers (Costco, Pace, Sam's Club) found that charging fees for their memberships generates customer loyalty. Shoppers apparently feel impelled to recover their membership costs through cost-saving purchases.[10]

Some service companies try to hold customers by making a move to a competitor too costly, complicated, or just plain time consuming. Let's say your stockbroker recommended buying Philip Morris just before it bellyflopped. This and other bad advice has made you decide to take your business elsewhere. Unfortunately, severing ties with an old broker isn't easy. Brokerage firms create unique products: in-house items such as mutual funds, limited partnerships, and annuities. You can't easily take these with you to another broker. Besides the time and effort involved, you could pay a penalty. Selling certain mutual funds, for example, before a deadline will trigger charges that run as much as 6 percent of the investment, definitely not small change.

Instead of penalizing a customer for leaving, frequent-customer programs provide a positive incentive to stay with a company. Choosing to continue to patronize a company because of the potential for future rewards is certainly different than being pressured into remaining a customer to avoid punishment. The additional goodwill and increased sales resulting from frequent-customer programs make this a popular approach across industries for keeping customers.

Service Wars
An entire town in upstate New York issues its own currency as a bartering system to reward and encourage local business.

Database Marketing

One of the first steps companies take before they start any major marketing strategy is to build huge lists of loyal buyers who can be regularly tapped for launching promotions and market research.

> The cost of holding a consumer's name, address, and purchase history on line has fallen by a factor of a thousand since 1970 and continues to fall at this rate. To appreciate the power of a customer database, one must see it not merely as a mailing list but as the memory of the customer relationship: a record of every message and response between the firm and each address. Add artificial intelligence and the system can design new messages, even product offerings, at the individual level to reflect everything learned from past interactions. When a low-cost computer drives a two-way communication medium this way, the result is an electronic marketer with as much flexibility as the average human salesperson, a better memory, and a talent for the most numbingly repetitive tasks.[11]

The key task in database marketing is to identify how individuals are different from others and then to use this knowledge to interact with them. In the 1970s, companies did not have the technology to discriminate in their mass mailings. As a result, we all got a lot of mail. We also became less indulgent about the impersonal promotions that overstuffed our mailboxes. We learned to ignore and throw away most of this junk mail.

In the 1970s and 80s, direct marketing took off. Ed McMahon offered us the chance to win $1 million. Publishers Clearing House gave away cars, boats, and houses to push their magazine subscription business. Big merchandisers like Sears, Spiegel, and L.L. Bean spent millions on direct mail efforts. Others like Avon, Hershey, and even Walt Disney became highly successful mail-order retailers.

This marketing-to-the-averages procedure has turned into a marketing-to-the-individual approach. The direct-marketing message is now much more personal. By storing information in a database and selecting out certain individuals, or family names, with 12 or 20 or 50 specific characteristics, companies send very individualized promotions. The products are also much more likely to interest customers. Many people appreciate information relating to their favorite foods, books, or even their current ailment.

 Database marketing is for retailers and other businesses wishing to maintain customer profiles to customize their products, services, and marketing efforts. Look under "data processing services" in the phone book.

An excellent application of database technology benefiting the customer is the development of customer history systems. The principle is the same: building a continuous relationship with each customer. Retailers and other businesses wishing to maintain customer profiles use these programs to build valuable stores of information that can be accessed to customize products, services, and marketing efforts.

For hotels, guest history programs capture a range of data and preferences. At Four Season's Hotels and Resorts, guest histories remember room-style preferences, rates paid, amenities, and special requests such as a stationary bicycle, high- versus low-floor rooms, and even meal preferences. These are used to create the best possible guest experience.

But guest histories go beyond simply knowing who dislikes feather pillows or who loves California chardonnay. They offer concrete business-building opportunities for boosting individual patronage, which has greater profit potential than group business, by targeting repeat customers or selecting the best candidates for certain promotional efforts. Inter-Continental's "Six Continent" guest recognition program tracks which guests spend more, eat in fine dining establishments instead of the coffee shop, buy suites, and use concierge, laundry, and valet services.[12] Targeted guests can be invited to arrive a night earlier or encouraged to stay over for a family-weekend package. Other customized benefits such as sending out birthday cards, offering other special amenities to guests or creating a no check-in procedure (pick up keys at a VIP station) can easily be created from these programs.

Service Wars
UNISYS targets
government agencies
with their service
technology.

cus•tom•er•ize \ kŭs'-tə-mə-rize' \ *vt*
1: to make a company more responsive
to its customers and better able to attract
new ones **2:** to customerize an organization's information strategy, e.g., to
extend systems capabilities to
field locations and other points of
customer contact and support **3:** what
Unisys Corporation does for a growing
roster of companies, and government
agencies, worldwide *syn* **see** CUSTOMER
SERVICE. COMPETITIVE EDGE. BUSINESS-
CRITICAL SOLUTIONS. REVENUE GENERATION

ARE YOU CUSTOMERIZED?

**1. Do you generate as much business
from each customer as you want?**
□ **Yes** □ **No**
A critical component of business
growth is increased sales content. To maximize each business opportunity, you need
a way to leverage your entire organization–
to bring it totally to bear at the point of
customer contact.

**2. Does your entire organization know
what your customers want?**
□ **Yes** □ **No**
A customer orientation has limited
value unless it's embedded in the very
fiber of an enterprise–at all levels, and at
every place that directly or indirectly
impacts the customer.

**3. Is your information strategy focused
on helping you hear what customers
and markets are trying to tell you?**
□ **Yes** □ **No**
The next best thing to reading your
customers' minds is listening to what
they're saying. But unless you're constantly
tuned in to customers' signals, you're missing messages that could guide you to
greater results for your business.

**4. Can your organization respond
quickly to what customers and markets
are telling you?**
□ **Yes** □ **No**
When the flow lines of your information system are not within your customers'
reach, you won't always sense when
opportunity knocks. But even if you do,
getting the message is not enough. If you
can't reply rapidly to market cues with
information, products and services, revenue opportunities are lost.

**5. Does your information strategy
enable you to proactively deliver
information to your customers?**
□ **Yes** □ **No**
Many business plans underestimate
the power of information to build
customer relationships. But imagine the
advantage of an information technology
strategy that transforms information into
customer-generating, revenue-generating
fuel.

**6. Are the full capabilities of your
organization accessible to your
customers at all your field locations?**
□ **Yes** □ **No**
An office. A branch. A retail site.
To a customer, that's your company. One
small part of the whole. Which is why you
need to leverage your entire organization
by extending its capabilities to each point
of customer contact.

**7. Does your information strategy
reflect the bottom-line importance of
customer service?**
□ **Yes** □ **No**
Business is built on customers.
Without them, there is no bottom line.
Government is also built on customers,
the public. And whether you're in the
business of commerce or the business of
government, no objective of an information strategy is more fundamental than
enhanced customer service.

The Bottom Line. *You might well agree
that this simple test suggests the enormous
advantages of becoming customerized.
Unisys will work with you to provide the
answers you need.*

Courtesy of Unisys Corporation, Blue Bell, PA.

Relationship Marketing

Frequent customer programs and database marketing efforts contribute to a more comprehensive approach to satisfying customers called *relationship marketing*. Relationship marketing depends on the goodwill generated by frequent-buying programs as well as on the information provided from database marketing efforts. Often, frequent-buyer program members are not loyal and will flee to another promotional program without hesitation. This is because these programs do not solve customer's problems or satisfy needs or wants.[13] Research by the U.S. travel data center found that these programs, by themselves, will not build true, enduring loyalty. Relationship marketing, on the other hand, goes beyond simple promotions or short-term awards and involves all the elements of a firm's products and services to encourage a personal relationship with each customer.

According to management at La Quinta Inns,[14] relationship marketing is "knowing the customer and using that information to bond with them." La Quinta's executives encourage property managers and front-desk clerks to get to know regular customers. They want the customer to be greeted as a friend upon arrival. The goal of their frequent-traveler club is to support this relationship. This program helps to form the initial personal contact and then serves as the foundation for nurturing this brief encounter into a friendly and accommodating relationship by focusing on personal guest information. In addition to knowing the purchase habits of members (room selection, certain amenity preferences, and so forth), personal information such as spouse's name and hobbies are added to a member database (see previous section on database marketing). The company uses this information to tailor special events and products to small segments of the membership.

La Quinta is seeking to increase this guest interface. Although their efforts in relationship marketing began with the frequent traveler club, La Quinta now sends guests a newsletter reporting on hotel events and promotions, and more important, provides special interest information tailored to various guest segments. The first issue targeted seniors and traveling salespersons, two prime guest markets for La Quinta. Dietary, transportation, sightseeing, and other travel information was included for seniors; and professional selling tips (e.g., "Zig Zigler's Selling Secrets") were added for salespeople. The salesperson's version is also available on audio cassette. This is a preferred format by salespeople because of the amount of time they spend in their cars.

Business can be lost if companies fail to communicate with their customers after a sale. A communications program that delivers useful information can nurture relationships with established customers. World-class companies maintain a mix of communications designed to inform, reassure, and keep their customers. (Methods of collecting customer feedback are listed in Exhibit 3–1.) There are many ways to promote customer loyalty through communication:

- *Fax updates to customers.*—Information generates ideas and ideas often turn into sales. Changes in products or services, technology, raw materials, legislation, and so on can be of real interest to customers and contribute to building relationships.
- *Send hand-written notes.*—Inform customers of new products, special sales, or scarce or limited offerings. Unless you have to reach thousands of customers, hand-written correspondence has extraordinary impact. Think of how you react when a person takes the time to send you a personal note.
- *Telephone your customers.*—Don't use prerecorded telephone devices that put customers on hold only to return with another recording. Have a manager or the customer's salesperson call. See if they are pleased with a recent purchase. Did it provide what they were looking for? If a top executive makes the call customers will feel very important. Customers are reluctant to leave a business if they feel they have a direct link to the boss.
- *Demonstrate two-way communication.*—A newsletter can be made different than the typical, boring trade magazine format. Include reader-response sections. Address reader concerns with follow-up material. Done properly it can create a sense of family between the business and key customers.[15]

The Ritz-Carlton Hotel Company recognizes that existing customers are a company's most-valued asset. They have identified the lofty goal of achieving 100 percent customer retention. *Zero defections* means keeping all the customers you can serve profitably, and not losing *any* you wish to keep. Most business must come from repurchases because there are not enough new customers available to support long-term success based on trial alone. Guest loyalty has had the single largest impact on their long-term market share growth.

The Ritz-Carlton Repeat Guest History Program (see Exhibit 6–5) is a model for the industry and plays an important role in their guest retention

EXHIBIT 6–5
The Ritz-Carlton Repeat Guest History Program

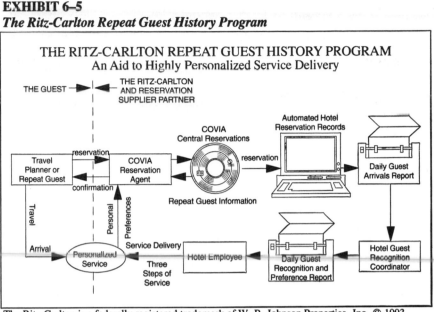

THE RITZ-CARLTON REPEAT GUEST HISTORY PROGRAM
An Aid to Highly Personalized Service Delivery

strategy. This system remembers a growing number of guest preferences and directs this information to the appropriate employees when guests return.

COMPLAINT MANAGEMENT

By maintaining frequent contact with customers, companies can perceive difficulties sooner and address small concerns before they become real problems.

What annoys you the most?

- Waiting in long lines while other windows or registers stay closed.
- Not having a table ready at the reserved dining time.
- Staying home for a delivery that fails to show.

If you picked any of these, you're like most Americans. Anything that wastes our time really ticks us off. Combine this with our intolerance for rudeness and it's not surprising that customer loyalty is rapidly disappearing. According to a *Wall Street Journal* survey, American's biggest complaints about service are "staying home for delivery", "salespeople who fail to show," and "a poorly informed salesperson who can't describe how a product works."[16]

Since the 1970s, when Ralph Nader led the consumer movement, customer complaints have increased. Organizations have responded by creating consumer affairs positions, elevating their departments, and installing toll-free numbers for countless situations. In 1990, the Society of Consumer Affairs Professionals had 600 corporate members; in 1993 it listed 1,400.

Although more companies are responding to and resolving consumer complaints, the difficulty involved in lodging a complaint still prevents most consumers from doing so. Companies should make it easy for dissatisfied customers to voice their disapproval. For example, the president of JP Hotels (14 Holiday Inn franchises) posts his home, office, and mobile telephone numbers in every room of each hotel and urges guests to call him with complaints. Several general managers at Embassy Suites hotels have their desks in the hotel lobby to handle guest problems and to stay in better touch with customers and staff.[17]

Service Wars
Procter & Gamble has an 800 number for customer service on every product it sells in the United States. Coca-Cola set up an 800 line after studies showed that only 1 unhappy person in 50 bothers to complain.

Let's look at an example of how important filing a complaint can be. Buying a new car is an extraordinary event. For many, driving home in a new automobile can be an exhilarating experience. It's a boost to our ego; part of the American dream, and a rite of passage into our upwardly mobile society. But it can turn into a horrifying experience. Persuasive salesmen, well-practiced finance managers, and pricing terms that appear favorable can push a customer into making an impulsive and bad decision. When the reality of the purchase becomes clear and the dissatisfied customer wishes to revise his or her decision, however, complaints are not easily registered.

Mazda, while known for its unique car designs, is similar to other car manufacturers in how it handles customer complaints. Although Mazda has an 800 customer service hot line, the corporation is not responsible for the behavior of individual Mazda dealers. The customer must stand alone in his or her dispute with the dealership. It's hard enough for a customer to file a complaint; but it's even worse when no one is willing to take any responsibility.

 *T*ake personal responsibility in trying to resolve complaints or to fulfill customer needs. Be accountable to the customer even when you are not directly responsible for the problem.

Few companies use or pay attention to complaints. Who wants to hear what they're doing wrong, especially if the criticism is well founded. It is estimated that 90 percent of dissatisfied customers whose problems were not solved will never do business with the retailers that sold them the product nor will they again buy the product that caused the problem.[18]

On a personal level we all know what our faults are but get defensive when they're pointed out. We're also aware of weaknesses in our job performance, problems in our organization and imperfections in its products and services. But reacting to criticism is difficult. We tend to respond in a guarded and defensive way, which may avoid squarely confronting the real problem. Likewise, companies tend to let themselves off the hook too easily: "We never could have satisfied *that* customer." More often than not, they fail to provide complainers with satisfactory responses. For example, although some auto dealers go through the motions of tracking customer comments, they refuse to believe the information obtained from the exercise.[19]

The astonishing news is that those people who do complain and have their problem taken care of tend to be more loyal to the company than the people who were satisfied in the first place.

 *W*orld-class companies see complaints as opportunities to improve, to impress customers, and to turn complaining customers into loyal ones.

The TARP Institute found that the return on investment for handling complaints far exceeds the consistent return of any more traditional investment (see Exhibit 6–6). The return on investment made in handling com-

EXHIBIT 6–6
Facts and Figures of Dissatisfied Customers

- 96 percent of dissatisfied customers do not complain to the company. For every 10 complaints there are 250 other dissatisfied customers.

- Dissatisfied customers tell 8 to 10 other people, twice as many as a contented customer tells about a pleasing experience.

- At any one time, 25 percent of customers are upset enough to switch to a competitor if there is a reasonable alternative.

- 90 percent of dissatisfied customers whose problems were not solved will never do business with that company again.

- 54 percent of those unhappy customers whose difficulties are resolved remain loyal to the merchant or brand name.

- The average return on investing money to handle complaints is approximately 170 percent.

- The direct costs of losing a customer over a 20-year period are $150,000 for auto manufacturers, $3,000 for appliance companies, $600 for banks, and $110,000 for supermarkets.

Source: The White House Office on Consumer Affairs; Technical Assistance Research Program (TARP) Institute, Consumer Complaint Handling in America: An Update Study, April 1, 1986, pp. 5–6.

plaints ranged from a low of about 15 percent for packaged goods firms to 100 percent for automotive and consumer durable companies. The results even showed that proper handling of complaints in the banking industry yielded a 170 percent return.[20]

Obviously organizations should strive to provide customers with no reason to complain in the first place. But when imperfection strikes, a well-crafted recovery process can turn a weakness into good business.

Some companies, however, assume that actively seeking customer complaints may create a negative image, reinforcing the fact that the company is in the wrong.[21] Do not avoid legitimate complaints. Ask customers what was wrong and what they liked about the purchase and your company.

At Procter & Gamble's Duncan Hines angel food cake factory in Jackson, Tennessee, line workers are given letters from customers who have problems with their product. One worker called up a customer whose angel food cake did not rise and helped figure out why by asking such questions as, "How long did you beat the mix?" and "What temperature did you bake it?" According to P&G's CEO, "What we've said to the

EXHIBIT 6–7
Guidelines for Complaint Management

- Provide a thorough response. Acknowledge, apologize, correct, and follow up—ensure the customer's satisfaction and root out the problem. Offer sufficient reimbursement and restitution. Errors in service require immediate response.
- Communicate customer feedback to employees. Solicit their assistance to resolve problems.
- Make your efforts efficient. Pareto analysis prioritizes customer complaints by frequency. It is based on an 80-20 rule of thumb: the majority of complaints come from a few specific areas. Efforts should be directed at the sources of the most frequent complaints. For example, Frito-Lay usually can pinpoint the 2 or 3 accounts responsible for the majority of customers complaining about stale potato chips.
- Use the Ishikawa approach, also called *cause and effect* or *fishbone analysis* (see Exhibit 5–2), to focus on underlying reasons for complaints. Often comment cards (complaint cards) can magnify problems.

worker is, this is the only place we make angel food cake, and you're responsible for it, and if you'd like to talk to the customer, we'd like you to talk to the customer."[22] This innovative idea costs only the time of the employees' calls.

 *C*ommunicate customer feedback to employees. Keep the personal comments private and make the public comments, good and bad, known to everyone.

Complaints can offer a variety of benefits to customers and organizations if managed properly. Exhibit 6–7 presents guidelines for handling customer complaints.

When customer complaints are received, responded to, and fixed, there is a 90 percent chance that the unhappy customers will return. Exhibit 6–8 presents an example of how a company should communicate with a dissatisfied customer. Responding to a complaint about a piece of wood found in their food product, this company apologized by sending a case of the product to the customer. Complaints also offer the obvious value of pinpointing areas that need to be improved. Taking even minor problems seriously allows an organization to show off its customer skills and actually benefit from the incident. Here's an example:

EXHIBIT 6–8
Sample Response Letter

Mr Nature.
"GOOD NUTS ARE GOOD HEALTH"®

December 3, 1993

Mr Jonathan D. Barsky, Ph.D.
UNIVERSITY OF SAN FRANCISCO
2130 Fulton Street
San Francisco, CA 94117-1080

Dear Mr Barsky:

All of us here at Mr. Nature would like to take this opportunity to express our sincere apology for your recent experience with our product. I would also like to thank you for bringing this to our attention.

We take the utmost care in processing and packaging our products to insure our customer's satisfaction. I requested that our quality control manager check into this matter.

As a small token of our appreciation we will be forwarding a case of Mr. Nature products to you. We hope that you will confident in our commitment to provide quality products to our customers.

Very truly yours,

MR. NATURE

Tammie C. Dubrowskij
Quality Control

TCD:tcd

1105 KEARNEY ST. • LOS ANGELES, CA 90033-2193 • (213) 268-2686 • FAX: (213) 268-5066 • TOLL FREE: 1-800-462-8873

One weekday morning, a young woman entered the Sheraton Palace Hotel in San Francisco and requested a nonsmoking room with a king-size bed. Luckily, one room fitting this description was available for that evening. It was approximately 11 AM and the woman had to attend a meeting. She requested the room be ready when she returned that afternoon, and the clerk confirmed that it would. After returning from the meeting at 5 PM, she found that the room had not been cleaned. Distraught, she exited the hotel and left a very stern message for the desk manager. She asserted that neither she nor her company would ever return to that hotel again.

The manager was not in the hotel the morning that she arrived. However, he did feel responsible and left a phone message for her at her office. Finally speaking with her, he apologized, admitted it was the hotel's fault, and offered her a marker for a free room. Several weeks later, she called and said that she could not find a hotel room for herself and a friend. Every hotel in the city was sold out because of a medical conference. The manager accommodated them both with two complimentary rooms for three nights. Since then, she has returned on eight separate occasions, and her company continues to provide a significant amount of business for the hotel.[23]

 Admit when you're wrong—make it clear, direct, and sincere. Then apologize, correct the error, and offer sufficient restitution.

SERVICE AND SATISFACTION GUARANTEES

Standing behind a restaurant meal, a car wash, or even a haircut with a clearly stated, hassle-free guarantee may be somewhat difficult to control, but it can offer a strong competitive advantage. It can be the needed extra for some customers, especially when previous experience has made them skeptical. Even high-risk or high-priced services such as financial investments, real estate, or insurance should provide, and can benefit from, guarantees. Service guarantees contribute significantly to building customer trust and loyalty even though their terms may be difficult to clarify.

*O*ffer a guarantee on your products and services—they're worth it.

Do Guarantees Pay Off?

Do customers exploit guarantees of service and satisfaction? Only five months after introducing it, Eastern Airlines canceled a program that offered passengers their money back for nearly any reason. Accepting even trivial complaints, such as the ice cream being too soft, made getting refunds too attractive for passengers to pass up. Federal Express has also returned millions of dollars to customers because it guarantees never to be even one minute late.

Service Wars
L.L. Bean thinks customer service is so important that it once sent a customer a new raft and $700 to pay for the fishing equipment he lost when his first L.L. Bean raft leaked.

But backing up products and services with a carefully crafted guarantee of refunds can be good business. "Whatever is refunded to disgruntled customers is offset by overall efficiencies in operations and by valuable information that otherwise might not have been brought to management's attention."[24]

These programs can either be the centerpiece of a service company's entire operation or simply a promotional tool. Many businesses continue to make shallow promises with slogans because they are not prepared to guarantee what their customers want. For a company serious about delivering on its promises, a guarantee may even help it focus on its customers. Hampton Inns' president R.E. Schultz believes that their service guarantee "not only helps to differentiate us from the competition, but is just as important to our employees as it is to our customers. A maid knows that if she doesn't clean a room right, someone will go down to the front desk and ask for a refund.[25] Franchisees recruit and train only those people who will carry out the service that the company promises. As a result, Hampton Inns reports that the number of customers invoking its guarantee is very low; so is the number of cheaters.

Banks have also embraced service guarantees, not only for their marketing appeal, but for their impact on organizational effectiveness. About 25 banks in the United States have made operational changes to commit themselves to a permanent promise of guaranteed service. For example, the "Oops!" program of Union National Bank and Trust Co. pays $5 for "any mistake of any kind that the bank makes." This program is unconditional, easy to invoke, and quick to pay. It is also highly successful because customers want the level of service promised, not the $5 that comes when a mistake is made. But most important, it has affected performance and reduced mistakes to one error in 7,000 transactions, a 99.9 percent accuracy rate.

 *O*ffer customers a guarantee that has real value. Make it unconditional, easy to invoke, and quick to pay.

Federal Express has returned millions of dollars to customers as a result of its guarantee never to be even one minute late. But, critics say the company doesn't take the term *guarantee* seriously enough. The policy won't be enforced unless the customers report the late shipment. Another delivery company, Guaranteed Overnight Delivery (GOD) automatically refunds money on any late delivery. Even refunds for late deliveries that would have gone unnoticed are credited to companies' accounts, which would certainly surprise some bookkeepers when they see the correction on their monthly statement. This is an excellent example of a truly hassle-free and forceful guarantee. Exhibit 6–9 presents guidelines for creating an effective guarantee.

Here is an example of a good 100 percent guarantee on a magazine subscription:

> We stand behind everything we publish. If you're not completely satisfied with our magazine, you may cancel at any time for a full, 100 percent refund of every cent you paid. Not a prorated refund, but a complete refund of your entire subscription price. No questions, no discussion, no problems.

Here is an example of a bad money-back guarantee:

> If you are not pleased with the return on investment you get from any ACE Productivity Center seminar, tell us why and we will refund up to 100 percent of the registration fee, no questions asked.

EXHIBIT 6–9
Guidelines for Creating a Quality Customer Guarantee

A quality guarantee is:

- Legitimate—Offer fair and sufficient coverage, not partial or too short-lived. Do whatever is necessary to provide customer comfort.
- Hassle-free—Make it easy to collect. Take complete responsibility for redeeming the guarantee payout.
- Distinct—Call it something special like, the "no-risk" guarantee.
- Forceful—Try a 45- or 60-day guarantee instead of the typical 30 days.
- Explicit—Spell out the guarantee. The more confidence you can give the potential buyer, the better. Avoid or minimize restrictions.
- Sincere—Don't use legal jargon or fine print. Also avoid asterisks.
- Obvious—Make it stand out. Print it large; put a border around it. Include the guarantee with your reply.

Source: Ivan Levinson & Associates, *The Levinson Letter*, 14 Los Cerros Drive, Greenbrae, CA 94904.

The problems with this bad guarantee are

- "Return on investment" is too ambiguous.
- A refund of "up to 100 percent" is also vague. How is this decided? Will they return only 5 or 10 percent?
- There is a contradiction: "tell us why" and "no questions asked." This makes the guarantee sound evasive and difficult to invoke. The good example, however, is very explicit about the no-questions-asked return policy.

It is especially difficult to guarantee intangible products, for instance, transportation, consulting, investment banking, or health care, that can't be experienced or tested in advance. "When prospective customers can't taste, test, feel, smell, or watch the product in operation in advance, what they are asked to buy are, simply, promises of satisfaction."[26] Sometimes it takes real imagination to create guarantees for products and services, as the following examples indicate:

- Jaguar now offers the "love" guarantee: "If you think that love isn't a sure thing, then you haven't driven a Jaguar." The company will fully refund your money if, for any reason, you don't love your Jaguar.

- Xerox's "Total Satisfaction Guarantee" now covers all the company's equipment. Xerox promises satisfaction with each product or it will replace the product free of charge for up to three years from the purchase date. According to a Xerox spokesperson: "We're putting the customer in charge. The customer is the sole arbiter and decision maker."[27]
- Crest involves its consumers and their dentists in a six-month promotion. If consumers aren't satisfied with the results of their examinations after using Crest for six months, they get their money back.[28]
- McDonald's now guarantees customer satisfaction and backs it up with a free meal. A customer's next meal is free if he or she is dissatisfied with the current meal. McDonald's will also fix anything wrong with current meal.
- Richard Chase, a professor at the University of Southern California, offers a satisfaction guarantee for his graduate course, "Management of Services." Although colleagues are scared they may be forced to do likewise, he has yet to have any student demand payment. Students must request any rebate before their final grade is issued.

A customer who exercises a guarantee or warranty is a complaining customer. Finding out why customers are invoking a guarantee is also very important so that patterns may be easily identified and corrected. But be careful not to violate the no-questions-asked clause of your guarantee. Each time someone collects on the guarantee, have either the customer or an employee fill out a brief card explaining the reason for the complaint. Do this after completing the refund process. However, it may not be evident to the employee why the customer is collecting on the guarantee; moreover, some customers may not provide any clue to explain their dissatisfaction.

Returned merchandise or requests for refunds should also be seen as complaints and offer similar opportunities to turn around the customer with world-class treatment. Even the mail-order guru L.L. Bean gets many complaints. But they take advantage of the potentially damaging situation. In 1988, dissatisfied customers returned $82 million worth of goods, 15 percent of all L.L. Bean's sales. The company's reaction was not to curtail its return policy but instead to identify the most frequent complaint (wrong size) and take corrective action (updating of size information in catalogs and in order-taking computers).

A customer who returns merchandise, requests a refund, or exercises a guarantee or warranty is a complaining customer. Value their input.

The internal guarantee.   The same idea of customer guarantee can be used to benefit internal customers.[29] There is often a lack of responsibility felt between departments or among employees on the same level. Mistakes sometimes occur because crucial deliveries or other procedures aren't adequately defined. Internal guarantees support corporate objectives such as quality and productivity.

In creating a service guarantee, employees must agree on specific performance details. This forms "the promise." The payout in an internal guarantee is different than in the consumer guarantee. Soft payouts are more appropriate in an internal guarantee; money is not appropriate. The emphasis should be on rewarding employees rather than punishing offenders. The payout could be having to pay for lunch, singing a song at a meeting, or so forth. Done correctly, internal guarantees can reduce the customer's need to invoke a consumer guarantee.

Warranties

Take responsibility for your products and services. More companies are separating liability and the obligation of standing behind their products and services. They are selling this responsibility as an additional service, instead of being automatically accountable for what they sell.

Although hardly new to marketing efforts, warranties are taking on a life of their own. More than simply representing a customer service or added value, these extras are a significant source of profit for many companies. Insuring products against breakdown is among the most lucrative ideas still left in retailing.

Americans spend about $5 billion each year on extended warranties, special insurance and service contracts; half of this is for coverage on new-car purchases. The problem is customers aren't getting their money's worth. Retailers are exploiting these add-ons. They are taking advantage of the abstract concept and confusing details of warranties and of customers' fear of the high technology in many new products.

Circuit City electronics obtains nearly half of their profits ($78 million net income in 1992) from selling extended service contracts. Macy's offers a five-year contract on electronics for $240 covering technical assistance, maintenance, repairs, and house calls. Friedman's Microwave Ovens makes a healthy profit from selling extended service contracts and charges only $1 per month. Some computer dealers offer extra warranties if the customer pays a 10 percent premium over the purchase price.

Many companies do offer legitimate warranties. When Compaq Computers decided to sell directly to customers to stay competitive with Dell and other mail-order computer retailers, it lowered its prices and introduced the industry's first long-term warranty. The coverage, three years (with minor exclusions), gives consumers more security and confidence in making a major purchase by mail.

Protection is now available for investment in a child's college tuition. Even weddings can be warranted against unexpected disaster, such as being called up for military duty (change of heart is *not* covered).

Warranties were originally intended to protect the integrity of products and to be accountable for repair and replacement of defective parts. Utilizing warranties as promotional and profit making tools is beneficial when they offer real value to customers and don't reduce the implicit responsibilities of the seller of products and services.

In addition, many credit cards now offer free extended warranties and some type of protection when purchases are made with their card. Most items are covered under the extended warranty (except, for example, cars, boats, or motorized equipment) and under the purchase security protection (except, for example, lost items or jewelry, watches, or other items stolen from the customer's car). They'll also double most manufacturers' warranties, adding up to one extra year of coverage, and include gifts under this protection. Although somewhat time-consuming to cash in on (for example, before collecting any money, the customer must show original store receipts), these enhancements are valuable marketing tools. The popularity of offering these services underscores the importance that customers place on this protection and the market value and economic viability of these added expenses. If credit card companies can benefit from covering your products and services, why can't you?

Frequent-user programs and product and service guarantees are two extremely effective ways to improve customer satisfaction. The secret lies in the low cost and high return obtained from investments directed at retaining loyal customers. Although processing complaints is easier with advances in technology, the real gains come from the insights they provide to improve operations and from the good chance of turning a complaining customer into a loyal fan.

SUMMARY

- The cost of retaining a loyal customer is only one-fifth that of attracting a new one.
- Frequent-user programs reward faithful customers and provide incentives to encourage repeat business.
- Create a frequent-customer program—but keep it simple.
- Offering customers recognition rewards is a low-cost, low-risk alternative to frequent-buyer programs that avoids a long-term investment.
- Database marketing is for retailers and other businesses wishing to maintain customer profiles to customize their products, services, and marketing efforts. Look under "data processing services" in the phone book.
- Take personal responsibility in trying to resolve complaints or to fulfill customer needs. Be accountable to the customer even when you are not directly responsible for the problem.
- World-class companies see complaints as opportunities to improve, to impress customers, and to turn complaining customers into loyal customers.
- Communicate customer feedback to employees. Keep the personal comments private and make the public comments, good and bad, known to everyone.
- Admit when you're wrong—make it clear, direct, and sincere. Then apologize, correct the error, and offer sufficient restitution.
- Offer a guarantee on your products and services—they're worth it.
- Offer customers a guarantee that has real value. Make it unconditional, easy to invoke, and quick to pay.
- A customer who returns merchandise, requests a refund, or exercises a guarantee or warranty is a complaining customer. Value their input.

NOTES

1. Daiann Irigoyan identified the various components of barriers to purchase as search costs, perceived risks, and lack of information.
2. George Brown, "Brand Loyalty—Fact or Fiction?" *Advertising Age,* June 19, 1952, pp. 53–55.
3. The problems of oversatisfying or creating expectation levels that may be difficult to meet are discussed later.
4. Richard L. Oliver and John E. Swan, "Consumer Perceptions of Interpersonal Equity and Satisfaction in Transactions: A Field Survey Approach," *Journal of Marketing* 53 (April 1989): p. 21.
5. From J. Heskett et al., *Service Breakthroughs* (New York: Free Press, 1990), p. 31.
6. In frequency programs, miles have proven to be the currency of choice.
7. James S. Hirsch, "More Hotels to Offer Plan for Air Miles," *The Wall Street Journal*, August 24, 1993, p. B1.
8. Donna Levine, "Rewarding Repeaters," *Restaurant Business*, August 10, 1988, p. 120.
9. A program's cost to higher-priced hotels is approximately $10 a stay according to Betsy O'Rourke, vice president, Choice Hotels.
10. "Shoppers Flock to Warehouses," *San Francisco Examiner*, August 2, 1992, p. E6.
11. Bill Moyers, *Healing and the Mind* (New York: Doubleday Publishers, 1993), p. 21.
12. As reported by John Cahill, senior vice president and manager of information services at Inter-Continental Hotels.
13. Robert Lewis and Richard Chambers, *Marketing Leadership in Hospitality* (New York: Van Nostrand Reinhold, 1989), p. 69.
14. Information provided by Isaac Jon Collazo, marketing information manager, La Quinta Motor Inns, Inc.
15. Mark Stevens, "Customer Communication Can Create Opportunities," *Star Tribune*, March 1, 1993, p. 70.
16. "The American Way of Buying," *The Wall Street Journal Centennial Edition*, June 23, 1989.
17. Bridget O'Brian, "Tracking Travel," *The Wall Street Journal*, July 10, 1992, p. B1.
18. Warren Brown, "The Selling of the Satisfied Customer," *Washington Business*, October 23, 1989, p. 16.
19. Ibid.

20. Technical Assistance Research Programs (TARP) Institute, *Consumer Complaint Handling in America: An Update Study*, April 1, 1986, pp. 5–6.

21. John R. Graham, "Soliciting Customer Complaints Can Backfire," *Marketing News*, October 15, 1990, p. 16.

22. Brian Dumaine, "P&G Rewrites the Marketing Rules," *Fortune*, November 6, 1989, pp. 34–48.

23. Scenario provided by Dan Woulette, front desk manager at the Sheraton Palace Hotel in San Francisco.

24. Martin Everett, "More Companies Are Gambling on Service Guarantees," *Sales and Marketing Management*, May 1990, p. 109.

25. Ibid., p. 105.

26. Theodore Levitt, *The Marketing Imagination*, (New York: Free Press, 1986), p. 25.

27. "Xerox Guarantees 'Total Satisfaction,' " *Marketing News*, October 15, 1990, p. 2.

28. Laura Bird, "Advertisers Seek to Save Brands, Keep Customers amid Price Cuts," *The Wall Street Journal*, April 21, pp. B1, B7.

29. Susan Greco, "The ABCs of Internal Guarantees", *Inc.*, March 1993, p. 29.

Chapter Seven

Trends
Customer-Driven Technology and the Challenge of Satisfying Customers Worldwide

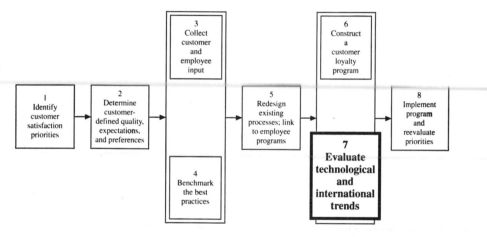

If a man carefully examines his thoughts, he will be surprised to find how much he lives in the future. His well-being is always ahead. Such a creature is probably immortal.

Ralph Waldo Emerson, *Journals*

The program outlined in Chapters 1–6 should help you tailor your organization to provide a satisfying customer experience. This includes mechanisms for assembling data, redesigning production and delivery, and achieving control and continuous improvement—all of which contribute to customer loyalty. These steps should be repeated for each work process and on a regular basis. This chapter will discuss how customer-driven organizations can integrate technological improvements and capitalize on international opportunities. World-class customer satisfaction depends on the wise use of technology and on the selective pursuit of developments in global markets.

CUSTOMER-DRIVEN TECHNOLOGY

You arrive at the hotel, pop your smart card in a doorway slot to introduce yourself, then go straight to your room, assigned earlier by computer. To enter, say your name, and the door automatically opens. You hang up your coat, punch in channel 162 on the TV, and hold a videoconference with colleagues. When the meeting ends, you flip to another channel to shop for a gift, then call home on the videophone to see how the family is faring while you are on the road.

This futuristic scene has arrived. Each component of this experience is currently available from at least one of the major U.S. hotel chains.

The hotel industry is not alone in its ability to affect the customer experience with high-tech applications. The U.S. economy could be in for a new era of economic growth as many businesses are embracing customer-oriented technology. Driven by changes in technology and management, increased productivity may set off a powerful cycle of fatter profits, new investment, higher wages, and a rising standard of living.[1] Seizing these opportunities builds from the topics discussed throughout this book. Improved customer technology may be necessary to deliver a redesigned work process with the required level of efficiency. Information technology such as user-friendly software, PC networks, handheld wireless terminals, and other gadgets are already moving information to factory floors and customer service departments to speed up and improve companies' responsiveness.

 *N*ew technology can attract customers, improve quality, and add value to their purchases.

These technological changes also result in impersonal service, job loss, and more complex problems that need quick resolution. Advances in technology don't always result in customer satisfaction.

EXHIBIT 7–1
Seven Sins of Phone Service

Companies fail when customers:
1. Have to listen to more than 10 rings (or no one answers);
2. Get a busy signal or are asked to hold by a machine.
3. Are placed in an excessively long hold cycle, or are simply ignored.
4. Get a message asking them to call back later.
5. Are told that the service representative will call them back.
6. Are passed around from one employee to another.
7. Receive an incorrect, inadequate, or impolite response.

Take, for example, the telephone. Phone systems are critical. They are one indicator of how important customer service is to a company. They reveal employee attitudes and how up to date the company is. Even production-oriented companies can lose business from not providing adequate phone service. But our comfort with traditional telephone service has created high expectations for new phone applications such as technical support hot lines, call distribution systems, and automated telemarketing. These approaches have, in some cases, not developed as fast as the technologies they support.

When customers call companies, only to be caught up in a web of electronic holds and transfers, they are frequently frustrated. In many instances the phone system is destined to fail. Exhibit 7–1 presents the seven sins of phone service.

For example, traditional PBX and key systems are designed with capacities just below peak demand levels so they may remain functional for the entire day. These systems cannot meet customer needs at certain times every day. The manufacturers, the telephone system salespeople and often the companies buying the systems are aware of this inadequacy. The problem is that many businesses have these dissatisfaction systems already integrated with their phone systems. This contributes to customer grief and aggravation on a daily basis. Mishandling of technology by management has occurred in many businesses. Technical innovation can outpace its ability to satisfy customers when managers misuse it, often in the name of short-term cost savings.

*C*ustomer satisfaction has to advance as fast as the technology it supports. Don't use new technology unless, without any doubt, it improves customer satisfaction.

The use of technical-support lines has also grown dramatically. The problem is that with few exceptions (most notably, WordPerfect Corporation and IBM Personal Computer Company) companies' toll-free customer-support lines are not handling the heavier traffic. This increased demand for help is not due to lower product quality. It's the result of inexperienced computer users needing more technical support and experienced users buying more technically advanced systems.

According to Labor Secretary Reich, "change simply isn't happening fast enough."[2] As a result, Reich backs a bill that would let his agency give grants and technical help to companies or unions to spread the word about how to involve workers in technological change. Stan Bromley, vice president of Four Seasons Hotels, also believes that companies are not responding quickly enough in meeting customer expectations: "With guests preferring high-tech services and often being dependent upon electronic information such as PCs, faxs, automated banking, and so forth, management has not reacted swiftly enough."

Despite their shortcomings, advances in phone technology offer tremendous opportunity to customers when managed properly. The problem is that many companies either don't know about these developments or are worried about their costs and complexity. There are numerous telephone-based technologies currently available that can markedly improve customer satisfaction and are within the budgets of even small businesses. We will look at these developments and examine some ambitious high-tech advances that will do wonders for boosting customer satisfaction in the future. The key is to determine how new technology will affect customer satisfaction and thus justify its costs. Organizations need to continually evaluate new technological opportunities based on this assessment.

Overall, telephone-based technology is developing rapidly to improve customer satisfaction. It is also becoming more accessible for small businesses.[3] For example, many companies have invested in voice processing, or voice mail which is a basic service useful for businesses of any size. Voice mail is a relatively inexpensive add-on to current telephone systems. Other advances in telephone-based technology offer tremendous potential to satisfy customers' needs and provide competitive advantages. Exhibit 7–2 details the features of a system used by hotels.

Another standard telephone technology for customer support is the automatic call distribution (ACD) system. This computer software system automatically distributes calls and provides customer support activities. For example:

Hello, you have reached XYZ company. If you have a touchtone phone press 1, now. (customer presses 1)

If you would like to speak with a customer service representative at any time during this message enter 0. (no response).

If you know the extension of the person you wish to speak with, enter this number now. (no response)

If you are calling about our weekend getaway to Bangkok, press 2 now. (no response)

If you are calling about our special balloon trip around the world, press 3 now. (customer enters 3)

This is called *conversant interactive voice response* . It enhances customer service by permitting quick response, complex services, and after-hours business. Detailed information can be provided to customers and orders can be taken 24 hours a day. It also offers the quick response of a small company and the advanced technology associated with a large company.

Although people are getting used to the impersonal aspects of this approach, the cardinal rule is to *always provide an early option of talking to a live operator*. At first, this will tie up many operators. As callers become more comfortable talking with a computer, they will select the live-operator option less. Voice-mail bashing will diminish as people realize how much time they can save and as the programs themselves improve.

The ACD phone system also tracks incoming calls, notes how long an operator is on each call, calculates the average wait time of a caller (until a real person answers), records how long each conversation takes, and offers analytical reporting capabilities. Local telephone companies carry this product.

Computer telephone integration (CTI) is another new development. If a customer calls L.L. Bean, for example, a representative will answer, "Hi (your name). How are you?" How did the employee know it was you? Dialing information is passed from your telephone to their PBX or key

EXHIBIT 7-2

Features of AT&T's Definity Communication Systems for Hotels

Guest Services

- Programmable wake-up calls and "do not disturb" commands.
- Private voice mailboxes with prompts in English, Spanish, and Japanese. Time zone adjustments made.
- Mailboxes and related message services that can be kept active for a period of time following checkout to allow, for example, a guest to check in for messages from the airport.
- Twelve presets for speed dialing of guest services and outside numbers (e.g., pizza delivery and emergency numbers).
- Portable computers on which to send and receive data.
- Speakerphone and conference call abilities.

Options

- Concierge support offers a menu of frequently requested information, then routes to appropriate employee.
- Ability to take and record room service breakfast requests, provide recorded announcements, and cover for employees who are away from their stations.
- Provides an easy way for guests to comment on hotel experience.
- Changeable recordings and digitized-speech answer calls, carry on a conversation, find out what information a guest seeks, access a database, and present the information to the guest in plain English.

Staff Services

- System linked with the property management system (PMS); requires only onetime data entry. For example, when a guest calls for service, his or her name is automatically displayed for personalized service. Direct input to PMS for systematic entry of guest information.
- Update room status from guest rooms or central location to permit accurate check-in.
- Without a PMS the telephone communication system still provides basic functions: room/maid status, check-in/check-out, and call restrictions.
- Instantly updates guest bill to reflect outside calls.
- Enhanced routing avoids local access charges.

Management Services

- Records guest requests and tracks staff and system responses to monitor and increase guest satisfaction.
- Auto call distribution system optimizes reservations, minimizes waiting time, and offers a variety of call-handling scenarios. Calls can be directed to three different stations during busy hours.
- Daily activity reports track use of system's features and overall system traffic. They help in employee scheduling and adjusting system for improved responsiveness.

Source: AT&T's Definity Communication System for the lodging industry and Rich Bassey, customer service specialist, AT&T.

system. Before the second ring, your call interacts with the company's computer and pulls up who you are and includes your full database of information. "How does your new red shirt fit?" This system, sort of a super caller ID, works only with customers who are already entered into the system. It doesn't work with new customers.[4]

Other developments to enhance customer service include:

- Still-image phone. These allow video frames to be sent over telephone wires to a video receiver.
- Cordless phones. These will become more popular. Expanded band width will eliminate all wires, in walls and on telephone poles.
- Tablet-size computers. Similar to the old game "Etch-a-sketch," these allow convenient ordering and inventory control. One can fax from tablet to warehouse. The benefit is less paperwork and better service. Previous orders can be called up. Icon-driven menus are easy to use.
- Videoconferencing. High-quality pictures by telephone lines will revive this underdeveloped opportunity for hotels. In-room videoconferencing may arrive at Marriott Hotels before the year 2000. Cheaper prices, larger screens, and multimedia capabilities will drive the battle for market share and gradually produce other improvements.
- *Business wire*. This is a new subscription service that sorts press releases pertaining to your industry and faxes them to you. It allows companies to keep up with current developments without having to actively search the Associated Press (AP) or United Press International (UPI) wire services.

Service Wars

At the Peninsula Hotel in New York, the concierge desk makes use of an airline ticket printer. Guests who need last-minute plane reservations can book flights and pick up their tickets right in the hotel.[5]

Other High Technology for Customers

During the 1970s and 80s, Japan's electronics makers followed a basic creed: new features sell products. They crammed stereos and radios with rows of buttons accompanied with thick instruction manuals. But starting in 1990, the motto became: the more user-friendly and simpler, the better. According to Matsushita president Akio Tanii, "We began to realize that there's a gap between what we've been making and what consumers want.'' Matsushita and other Japanese companies are using new technology to streamline how their products work. Even Matsushita concedes that technology hasn't developed far enough to make products truly simple.

Service Wars

The watch-size videophone—just like the one comic strip detective Dick Tracy has been using for years—was recently developed by scientists at Scotland's University of Edinburgh. They expect $10 million in revenue over the next five years for this fantasy-like product.

The Japanese may have had the lion's share of electronic innovation over the past three decades, but American ingenuity is taking back some ground from the Japanese in consumer electronics, pagers, and printer markets. For example, Quadlux, a Fremont, California, company, has invented what may be the next generation of microwave ovens and in some cases, even a replacement for conventional ovens. Their invention can cook with the speed of a microwave and provide the quality of a conventional oven. Called FlashBake, the device has the potential to increase restaurant production of pizzas and other dishes five to tenfold.[6]

The United States is also advancing with interactive and multimedia technology. Interactive communication allows consumers to do almost anything—shop, order from a selection of hundreds of movies, make phone calls, play games, or pay bills—on their TV sets. In 1993 AT&T concluded a two-year secret research project testing a variety of interactive and multimedia services. They concluded that the new services will have to be mindlessly simple to operate and must be presented as an advanced form of TV entertainment. They also determined that consumers will not use modified PCs for interactive operations.[7]

Travel agents now have access to all rates for all rooms (with a complete description of the room) in certain hotel chains, thanks to a joint technological development from Covia Corporation and Radisson Hotels International. ''Roommaster Inside Availability'' on the Apollo computer reservation system (CRS) is faster and more accurate than any previous system available to travel agents.

Some golfers now reserve tee times by dialing a computer and following the voice prompts. After the game, players enter their scores on-line to a database of prior scores and calculate a new handicap in seconds. Devel-

EXHIBIT 7–3
Guidelines for Going High-Tech

- Seek government assistance in upgrading your customer technologies. Call your local chamber of commerce regarding local, state, and federal tax incentives.
- Call the local telephone company about new technologies. ACD is the standard call distribution and customer support technology.
- Have customers help you decide what to buy. What technologies are they familiar with? Like? Dislike? Don't avoid brand new technologies. Evaluate their potential impact on customers.
- Introduce technical services incrementally to identify use patterns and determine procedures and future purchases.
- Test telephone technologies routinely to assess their ability to handle changing levels of demand. Customer service capacities should be programmed to accommodate peak levels.
- Use technology to reduce international trade barriers.

Lee Dahringer, "Marketing Services Internationally," *Journal of Services Marketing*, Summer 1991, pp. 5–17.

opments in expert software systems and image processing shorten the time a customer has to spend on the phone with a company and provide more information.

These convenience technologies, although necessary for maintaining market share, are likely to pale in comparison to the breakthrough satisfiers of the future that will exceed customer expectations in any number of product and service dimensions. Organizations need to continually evaluate new technological opportunities. See Exhibit 7–3 for prudent approaches to going high-tech.

Technological advances are originating in many different countries and are supporting the growth of global consumer markets. Despite the challenges of selling globally, the sudden opening of many markets and the competitive environment require swift action in order to seize these opportunities.

THE INTERNATIONAL CUSTOMER

Customer satisfaction throughout the world will continue to be affected by intense competition from Europe and the Pacific Rim. The changes caused by this competition (e.g., decreasing brand loyalties) will emphasize the importance of customer satisfaction as a strategic weapon, especially in the auto industry, consumer electronics, and consumer services.

Consumer sectors, lagging in productivity gains, will be pushed especially hard to improve as a result of this new global competition. European companies are expected to make big jumps in the quality of their services.

 *I*t is predicted that in two years European firms will actually overtake U.S. firms in customer service.[8] Benchmark the leading European companies now.

Asia will also contribute to service quality and innovation. Asian hotel companies, for example, will introduce new levels of customer service not familiar to U.S. consumers. And as other parts of the world begin to experience their newly liberalized economies, diverse and new approaches toward customer satisfaction will emerge.

Europe

The European Union is anything but a common market. Although economic and political barriers have been reduced, social and cultural differences remain. There are nine different languages and each country maintains distinctive national customs—for example, the British still take their coffee with milk and the French like their coffee black.

One effort to deal with the diversity of European business is ISO 9000, a quality standards certification program administered by the International Standards Organization in Geneva. Although initially designed for manufacturing companies in Europe, other versions of the certification are being developed to accommodate a variety of service businesses. The intent of ISO 9000 is to create standards for products traded across international borders and within the European Economic Union.

The ISO 9000 certification program, like other quality programs such as the Malcolm Baldrige Award, Six Sigma, and the Shingo Prize, requires customer satisfaction research. The standards list three primary objectives for organizations: (1) to achieve and sustain the quality of the product or service produced to continuously meet the purchaser's needs; (2) to give management confidence that the intended quality will be achieved; and (3) to give the purchaser confidence that the intended quality will be achieved. The certification also requires a written policy that lets others know about the company's commitment to total quality. The lesson for foreign companies wishing to do business in Europe is to prepare now for complying with ISO 9000 standards.

Companies trying to satisfy European customers must consider these differences and an assortment of local laws. These laws can range from stiff import quotas and local content requirements to a multitude of marketing regulations. Advertising liquor, for example, is prohibited in Ireland but is OK in Spain, if it contains less than 23 percent alcohol and is promoted after 9:30 PM. There is no commercial TV or radio in Sweden, and ads are permitted for only one hour on German networks. In Holland, ads for sweets must show a toothbrush in the corner of the TV screen. Each country has maintained most of its own market regulations, despite attempts to standardize trade practices.

The same challenges to achieving customer satisfaction in domestic markets extend to other countries. In Europe, TARP reports that for every customer who complains, 26 others remain silent, and that the cost of attracting a new European customer is five times the amount of keeping an old one. Similar results have been found to be true of U.S. consumers (refer to Chapter 6). But many Europeans consider customer complaints a bad thing, and customer service employees are afraid that blame will be placed on them for even taking the call of a dissatisfied customer.

On the other hand, in their European operations, Hewlett-Packard bases most of its decision making on the results of customer surveys. The company has successfully addressed the problem of complaints by aggressively soliciting feedback. A combination of customer feedback, customer satisfaction surveys, and total quality control compose Hewlett-Packard's customer satisfaction program in Europe. (These same approaches are supported and covered in Chapters 2 and 3.)

Asia

Japan, Hong Kong, Singapore, and other Asian nations will, however, be the toughest competitors in the race to gain a share in the global market for customer services. This competition will intensify as cash-rich Asian hotels, banks, and retailers increasingly enter U.S. and world markets. The U.S. government recognizes this and wants trade barriers to services discussed at international trade negotiations.

Asian approaches to customer service will accompany their growing investments and increase the level of competition to satisfy customers.

There are lessons to be learned from the Asians' employee allegiance and productivity. Companies must consider these, along with cultural differences, as more Asian companies expand their service operations.

 The principal advantages of the approach found in some Asian countries is that they consider jobs as careers, are courteous to strangers, emphasize attention to detail, and most important, believe that promoting the fortunes of their employer advances their own.

One of the keys to Japan's unprecedented customer satisfaction achievements is its skillful use of marketing. They know how to select a market, enter it the right way, build market share, and protect that share against competitors.

First, they find markets that need their skills, are receptive to standardized products, and have an oversized or complacent market leader. The U.S. auto industry fits that bill. Next, they build demand in unsatisfied market niches by advertising their products as low-priced versions of the leading brands. They are willing to wait before realizing a profit. The U.S. consumer electronics industry fell victim to this approach. After gaining a foothold in the market, they target their customers with product improvements and market segmentation. As they become market leaders, they continue to focus on the customer with continuous product development and refined market segmentation. This strategy is working as the Japanese are now making strong inroads into U.S. tire, machine tool, investment banking, hotel, and even food industries.

Some of Japan's global success is due to the help they get from their government, trading companies, and banks. Even though many businesses are also helped by low wage rates and unfair dumping, the real credit for success belongs to their unique business and management practices. Japanese management approaches have been difficult to execute in the United States, but we can learn much from their approach to customer service and satisfaction.

Theory S has been promoted as the U.S./Asian hybrid version of service. Similar to William Ouchi's theory Z, this approach suggests that capitalizing on the best of both cultures will improve performance. Japanese hotels, for example, in some ways deliver superior customer service than do U.S. hotels. This is not due to low labor costs or cultural differences. It is due to their ability to target specific guest needs such as offering business guests desktop computers with fax, telex, and word-processing capabilities and making checkout more comfortable with the use of guest lounges. This targeted approach can have a big impact on guest satisfaction and repeat patronage.[9]

Texas Instruments (TI) is also using this individualized approach to attract business by focusing on high-margin products. TI has moved away from catalog sales by tailoring products to fill the special needs of big customers such as Sony, Ericsson, and Sun Microsystems. They have created joint-development programs with these corporate clients in Europe and Asia by limiting their efforts to specialty chips. In this way, they are forging long-term business relationships with their international customers.[10]

China represents the last major market frontier on the planet. With all the potential, however, there are steep hurdles to satisfying the Chinese. An abysmal infrastructure can slow down the transport of almost anything; getting or delivering supplies can be a logistical nightmare. Given nonexistent research and the dramatic rise in incomes, no one has any idea of "how much soap can be sold" in China. Nonetheless, big consumer-products makers around the world are rushing to start, or in some cases expand, operations in the country that is home to nearly one quarter of the world's consumers.

The Rest of the World

Customer Satisfaction Measurement (CSM) Worldwide, a division of the Walker Group in Indianapolis, measures customer satisfaction in 35 countries in Europe, Asia, Australia, and North and South America. The company has also completed the first customer satisfaction measurement program in China. This was extremely difficult in a marketplace that, until very recently, had no concept of customer satisfaction whatsoever. Public exposure of employees who provide the worst service has been used by the Chinese to shame workers into improving service. Data gathered by CSM's affiliate companies throughout the world are entered into a database, which is available to all members. Having access to this data allows companies to compare their results with other companies within their country or with competitors around the world.

Beyond the obvious task of translating materials into other languages, CSM takes additional steps to compensate for different cultural values. Americans and Canadians, for example, are more enthusiastic than their

European counterparts. North Americans often describe things in superlatives: "great," "excellent," or "wonderful." Someone in Great Britain or Germany experiencing the same service and being equally satisfied with it might call it "fair" or "OK." CSM Worldwide adjusts the data so that international comparisons can be made.[11]

In many countries, customer satisfaction is rarely used as an effective marketing tool. Typically, conditions in many regions (most of South America, Africa, the Middle East, Russia, Eastern Europe, and much of Asia) are dictated more by daily pressures of supply and demand. Consumers have considerably fewer options and purchase primarily on the basis of need, price, and availability. This would appear to make our notion of customer satisfaction seem irrelevant. Economic, social, and political pressures quickly take precedence over efforts to find product and consumer niches or to heighten consumer pleasure with innovative services. Anyone who has traveled to Europe, China, Russia, Africa, or South America would agree that standards for measuring customer satisfaction are not the same for each country.

A well-focused, customer-oriented approach is essential in international markets. Satisfying customers is really a basic notion applicable to any economic market, social strata, or geographic location. But companies must customize for specific segments. In large international markets, success will come to those companies that not only offer customer-oriented products and services but that also find opportunities to sell to similar segments throughout the globe. Only in this way can economies of scale be achieved to keep costs competitive.

Another problem in pleasing customers in foreign markets is experienced first-hand by international travelers: fluctuating monetary exchange rates. These rates change daily in many countries and can shift radically during periods of economic turbulence. In Mexico, for example, when the peso was devalued to 150 pesos to the dollar, the price of a hotel room stayed the same for an American but the Mexican price tripled. Mexican incomes did not triple and thus Mexicans were shut out of their own market. Mexico or any other country can be either a bargain or very expensive depending on the exchange rate. Balancing exchange rates is a full-time occupation for any company that operates internationally. A principal concern of companies dealing with a variety of currencies is pricing both for the natives of a host country and for their international customers. By establishing some degree of presence, particularly in manufacturing, in your client's country, the costs of monetary exchange can be minimized. Service businesses can minimize the effects of monetary exchange by accepting flexible margins, engaging in hedging techniques, and maintaining a diversity of clientele.

Success in international markets depends on a thorough customer orientation, finding opportunities to sell to similar segments throughout the globe, and minimizing the effects of fluctuating monetary exchange rates with flexible margins, hedging techniques, and a diverse clientele.

THE FUTURE—RISING PRODUCTIVITY AND EXPECTATIONS

Many U.S. businesses are dependent on a shrinking pool of workers for jobs critical in providing customer satisfaction. These workers—from motivated frontline service workers to managers who can handle the new responsibilities that come with empowerment—will be in high demand. Significant productivity increases could satisfy part of the increasing demand for skilled labor, but forecasts call for 10 million new jobs in the U.S. service sector before the year 2000.[12] Unless a larger proportion of the labor force is equipped for these jobs, critical labor shortages will develop.

Goals 2000: Educate America, a federal program aimed at improving the quality of U.S. education, is intended to address these labor shortages. In addition to creating basic educational standards for schools and designating money to implement reforms, the legislation will create a National Skills Standards Board to certify workers in various jobs. This compentency-based evaluation system will establish voluntary standards for workers within targeted industries. Long-term goals include the linking of educational standards with the competency-based industry standards to reduce skilled-labor shortages and to strengthen overall global competitiveness.

It is no coincidence that the labor shortages are occurring at the same time that public education continues to be attacked for its failure to produce people qualified for these positions. Despite the lofty mission of the government's Goals 2000 programs, business will need to take a greater

EXHIBIT 7–4
Customer Satisfaction Resources

- American Marketing Association (AMA), Suite 200, 250 South Wacker Dr., Chicago, IL 60606, (312) 648-0536—The AMA's Professional Interest Groups include services marketing, business-to-business marketing, marketing research, health care marketing, sales/marketing management, and global marketing. Each may be reached through AMA's headquarters.
- International Customer Service Association (ICSA), 401 North Michigan Ave., Chicago, IL 60611-4267, (312) 321-6800—Membership required (approximately $200); benefits include networking with members and discounts on publications, such as customer service benchmarking surveys. Open to management and above.
- Technical Assistance Research Program (TARP), 1600 Wilson Blvd., Arlington, VA 22209, (703) 524-1456.
- International Quality and Productivity Center, PO Box 43155, Upper Montclair, NJ 07043-7155, (800) 882-8684—Call regarding specialized conferences on such topics as TQM, health care, and pharmaceuticals. Ask to be placed on their mailing list.

role in supporting and determining the scope of public education to keep up with skilled-labor requirements. Companies will be forced to take on more of this responsibility by investing in their own programs to develop workers and managers.

The need for more skilled employees comes from the growing consumer demands placed on business. This is the result of rising consumer expectations. New and changing consumer demands require a highly innovative and skilled workforce. We have become accustomed to next-generation software, new-product development, and dramatic medical advances. Our demand for the video phone is the result of our recent experiences with TV and instant telephone communications. Superfast trains and jet travel imply even greater expectations about travel in the future.

This notion of advancing just to keep up is essential in satisfying customers. It requires understanding past and current reactions to products and services by staying in touch with customers, employees, and competitors. Only by knowing customers and being sensitive to their preferences can companies anticipate and meet future customer expectations.

Exhibit 7–4 presents a list of sources of information about customer satisfaction.

SUMMARY

- New technology can attract customers, improve quality, and add value to their purchases.
- Customer satisfaction has to advance as fast as the technology it supports. Don't use new technology unless, without any doubt, it improves customer satisfaction.
- It is predicted that in two years European firms will actually overtake U.S. firms in customer service. Benchmark the leading European companies now.
- The principal advantages of the Asian approach is that they consider jobs as careers, are courteous to strangers, emphasize attention to detail, and most important, believe that promoting the fortunes of their employer advances their own.
- Success in international markets depends on a thorough customer orientation, finding opportunities to sell to similar segments throughout the globe, and minimizing the effects of fluctuating monetary exchange rates with flexible margins, hedging techniques, and a diverse clientele.

NOTES

1. "The Technology Payoff," *Business Week*, June 14, 1993, pp. 57–58.
2. Fred R. Bleakley, "The Best Laid Plans," *The Wall Street Journal*, July 6, 1993, p. 1.
3. This section is based on discussions and materials provided by Rich Bassey, customer service specialist, AT&T.
4. Michigan Bell now offers caller ID that accesses all the names as they appear in the phone book. This assumes that you have a display and that the caller is listed in the directory.
5. James Carper, "What Struck My Fancy," *Hotels*, January 1993, p. 11.
6. Michael J. Ybarra, "Costly New Oven Challenges Microwave," *The Wall Street Journal*, July 13, 1993, p. B1.
7. John Keller, "AT&T's Secret Multimedia Trials Offer Clues to Capturing Interactive Audiences," *The Wall Street Journal*, July 28, 1993, p. B1.
8. Based on a TARP study focusing on customer service complaints over a 20-year period in the United States and Europe.

9. Jonathan Barsky, "Theory S: Total Customer Service," *The Cornell Hotel and Restaurant Administration Quarterly*, May 1990, pg. 88–92.

10. "TI Is Moving Up in the World," *Business Week*, Aug. 2, 1993, p. 47.

11. Tawn Parent, "A Worldly Approach: Walker Group Takes Customer Satisfaction Measures Overseas," *Indianapolis Business Journal*, February 15, 1993, p 1.

12. James Heskett, W. Sasser, and C. Hart, *Service Breakthroughs* (New York: Free Press, 1990), p. 250.

Chapter Eight

Delivering World-Class Performance
Eight Steps toward Customer Satisfaction

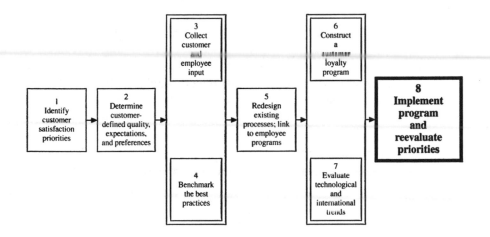

As I grow older, I pay less attention to what men say. I just watch what they do.

Andrew Carnegie

The purpose of this book is to bring together the ideas and techniques that are currently helping world-class companies to prosper. Although the size and scope of these approaches vary, common to all of them is the dedication to change.

Companies are making innovation a systematic process. The pace of change in business is increasing at an extraordinary rate. Global markets, technology, competitive forces, and demanding customers are exponentially transforming the way we live and work. This has contributed to a powerful climate of change, resulting in an unprecedented willingness of businesses to undergo radical transformations. Leading U.S. companies are making sweeping changes in their outlook, organization, and operation.

Some companies have pursued the most important change, improving customer satisfaction, with considerable fervor. But many organizations still dedicate most of their efforts to technical advancements and reducing expenses. Product development and leaner budgets are important, but "world-class cost and quality are merely the ante—the price of being in the game at all."[1] Only by understanding customers better than anyone else and translating this information into superior product designs, features, and after-sales support can companies expect to compete in today's intensely aggressive markets.

Companies need detailed information about customers; they must then coordinate their strategic reaction to this data throughout all their organizational levels. This approach to change makes the customer the focus of attention. The difficulty is building this response system. It often requires a series of conceptual leaps to go from facts about the customer to specific changes in products and services.

The supermarket industry, for example, has developed a model system whose principles can be applied to virtually every business. Efficient consumer response (ECR) uses customer information for affecting change throughout the entire grocery distribution supply chain. It forces traditional logistics, sales, and marketing functions into a systematic realignment throughout the channel for the purpose of increasing customer satisfaction. But even market intelligence that is well integrated with product and service design may not be enough. Success will come to those companies that look beyond traditional product definitions to the customer processes that will dictate the design of products and services in the future.

Understanding the customer is difficult. Anticipating the customer is essential. The complexity of consumer demand as well as shifts in basic supplier and labor relationships have caused businesses to reach out for programs that will help control these changes. Countless new approaches designed to respond to these new demands, such as total quality management (TQM), although effective in improving certain organizational functions, do not address all of the issues involved in achieving excellence and profitability in today's fast-paced climate. Other new ideas designed to fill these gaps (e.g., interactive planning, the viable systems model, socio-technical systems, systems dynamics, and organizational learning) also pursue business objectives with a limited, myopic approach.

Not only have companies lost out in their search for a management panacea, but so have their employees. The restricted approaches of many organizations pursuing change have left employees on all levels floundering in situations, causing stress and confusion. Organizations can only make effective change if they skillfully honor and acknowledge the needs of their employees. Organizations that help employees understand what is going on during organizational change can enhance employees' personal and professional growth, add value to their lives, and increase loyalty. These organizations will increase the effectiveness of the changes and improve their long-term impact.

The following *World-Class Customer Satisfaction Program* includes the best practices from U.S. and international businesses, universities, and government agencies. Although not a management cure-all, the program provides sufficient flexibility for your business to construct a unique approach to building customer satisfaction.

The principal features of this program are its comprehensive approach, adaptability to any size or level project, and reliance on continuous improvement. To be most effective, the program must be repeated on a regular basis. This means aggressively seeking customer, employee, and competitor input as part of an ongoing customer satisfaction strategy.

The program can be adapted to any operation, regardless of sales volume, number of employees, type of product or service, organizational structure, or location. Tailored to your organization, this integrated sequence of exercises links the latest developments in marketing, operations, and human resources for the exclusive purpose of achieving customer satisfaction and retention.

The logic of this program is simple. Profits come from loyal, satisfied customers. Customer satisfaction and loyalty are the result of exceeding expectations, especially in the areas most important to your customers. Exceeding expectations, in turn, is directly affected by both employee satisfaction and efficient operations. Employees who are carefully selected, well-trained, and motivated will require less supervision and be more productive in a well-designed operation. Policies and procedures that reflect an obligation to serve customers help employees to deliver this commitment.

The Preliminary Step begins your program with an overall assessment. Customer input will help to set your priorities; it will help you focus your efforts on areas likely to have the biggest impact on customer satisfaction. A new scoring system will help pinpoint the strengths and weaknesses of your products and services. You'll select a project and goal to pursue.

Customer priorities, expectations, and perceptions of quality will be assessed and merged within your strategy. Additional feedback will be obtained from customers and employees, focusing directly on your project's goal. Through benchmarking techniques, you will gather leading examples of how to resolve current failings and of new opportunities to excel. Then, by integrating all this information you will redesign your customers' experience and develop or adapt innovative human resource programs to support your new process.

To secure and capitalize on these efforts, you will create a customer loyalty program. The last step will consider how technology and global opportunities can enhance your customers' satisfaction.

THE WORLD-CLASS CUSTOMER SATISFACTION PROGRAM

This program is designed to apply the materials and concepts presented in Chapters 1-7 to your organization. This exercise is appropriate for projects of varying proportions and is equally suitable for an individual, a work team, department, division, or entire company.

Estimate a time frame in weeks for each step based on the number of employees affected. Approximate time frames are provided below. Read through each step as you get to it—then, give yourself a deadline. Revise these estimates as you progress. The World-Class Customer Satisfaction Program includes eight steps. Each step corresponds to a chapter in the book. For clarification of material, refer to the appropriate chapter.

Judgment Call

The actions recommended throughout this chapter need to be adapted to your situation. Most of these activities may be followed without modification. Certain directions, however, will require more creativity to suit your needs. The actions requiring *judgment calls* are noted with a scales icon, as shown here.

Steps	Time Estimate (range)	Deadline
Preliminary Step—Customers determine your overall strengths and weaknesses.*	(2–3 weeks)	
Step 1—Identify your objective with management feedback.	(1/2 week)	
Step 2—Apply the ingredients of customer satisfaction.	(1/2 week)	
Step 3—Integrate customer and employee input.	(1–2 weeks)	
Step 4—Benchmark for competitive advantage.	(1–2 weeks)	
Step 5—Redesign customer process; match with employee programs.	(1–2 weeks)	
Step 6—Develop customer loyalty with a frequent buyer program and a satisfaction guarantee.	(1–2 weeks)	
Step 7—Evaluate new customer technology and global opportunities.	(1–2 weeks)	
Total	(9–17 weeks)	End Date

Time frame estimates for complete program: 1–3 employees, 11 weeks; 4–19, 12 weeks; 20–50, 13 weeks; 51–100, 14 weeks; 101–250, 15 weeks; over 250 employees, 16+ weeks.

*For clarification of material in this step, see Chapter 3.

Preliminary Step

The purpose of this step is to conduct a general survey to identify which areas need improvement. You will:

- Estimate the typical customer cycle.
- Write a general customer survey.
- Select the sample and implement survey.
- Analyze the responses and find the general focus for program.

Your time frame: _____ weeks. Your deadline: _____.

   I. Current information.   This involves answering the following questions:

- What particular department, area, or product will be the scope of this program?
- From your experience, do you have a feeling for what the potential problem areas are?
- Talk with one manager and one frontline employee from this area about the potential problem. What are their reactions?
- Ask the manager, or anyone who knows, to identify the current customer mix for the product or service identified above.

II. Plan.   You will obtain information for this Preliminary Step through a customer survey (phone, mail, or in person). To develop this survey, first think of the sequence of steps taken by the customer—how the customer typically interacts with your products and services. Draw these steps in chronological order.

Start with a customer's first contact with your organization (products, advertisements, and so forth). All together, these steps should depict the complete consumption experience of a typical customer. However, if customers normally experience a variety of products and services, make sure to include the most frequently used ones as separate steps in this cycle. You may need to consult an employee who is familiar with the usage patterns of the various products and services encountered in this cycle. The last steps should represent any after-purchase contacts or any products or materials left in the customer's possesion.

If customer segments interact in very different ways, you may wish to isolate one segment and construct its unique customer cycle. An important consideration is to select the cycle that you believe has the greatest room for improvement, that offers the biggest potential gain for your organization.

Judgment Call

Write a one-page customer survey based on these customer steps. Use the following format:

Broad Scope Example

Expectations Met					Importance			
Not at all		*Exceeded*			*Low*			*High*
1	2	<u>3</u>	4	Check-in	1	2	<u>3</u>	4
1	2	<u>3</u>	4	Room	1	2	<u>3</u>	4
1	2	<u>3</u>	4	Food and beverage	1	2	<u>3</u>	4
<u>1</u>	2	3	4	Parking	1	2	3	<u>4</u>

Note: Each attribute (check-in, room, etc.) should relate to one customer step.

Narrow Scope Example

Expectations Met					Importance			
Not at all		Exceeded			Low			High
1	2	3	4	Reservations	1	2	3	4
1	2	3	4	Airport welcome	1	2	3	4
1	2	3	4	Check in	1	2	3	4
1	2	3	4	Room cleanliness	1	2	3	4

For detailed guidelines to construct your survey, refer to Exhibits 3–1 and 3–2. Do not include price, value, or other broad questions ("Overall, were you satisfied?") in the survey. These customer perceptions are affected by a variety of products and services. Instead, focus on individual customer steps (e.g., arrival, telephone systems, billing, complaint handling).

III. Implement

a. Sample selection. First, identify the total customer population that will be affected by the subject of this project. For example: all customers, business travelers, frequent customers, weekend customers. How will you reach these customers? In-person survey? Mail survey? Telephone survey?

You will need a minimum of 35 completed surveys for statistical reasons, but for our purposes 100 is preferred. The goal is to obtain between 35 and 100 completed surveys. What is the target number for your survey? How many must you distribute to get back this number of completed surveys?

Example: If you expect 80 percent to be returned and you wish to receive 100 completed surveys, then you must distribute 125 surveys.

$$1/\,80\% \quad \times \quad 100 \quad = \quad 125$$

return rate	desired number of completed surveys	total number needed to distribute

We recommend using the quality sample approach: try to obtain 100 percent return rate by providing incentives (Exhibit 3–3).

b. Survey distribution. The idea is to distribute the surveys proportionally across all market segments. You already estimated your current customer mix (Part I of this step). Multiply these percentages by the total number of surveys to be distributed. This is the number of surveys that need to be distributed to each of the corresponding market segments.

- How will you ensure a random sample (e.g., every third customer will receive a survey; each customer wearing blue; the fifth person appearing on each page of a customer list)?
- How will you ensure that the correct number of surveys will be distributed to each market segment?
- What incentives will you offer to improve the response rate?
- As the forms are completed, securely store the surveys (e.g., in a locked file or immediately delivered to a manager's office). Only after you have received your target number of completed surveys can you begin to evaluate the results. Set a cut-off date for accepting surveys that fits your overall time frame for this program.

c. Survey analysis. Use the survey responses to (1) figure out customer satisfaction (CS) scores for each question; (2) organize the comments that customers wrote on the surveys; and (3) see why some customers are not likely to return (repurchase). A computer is helpful, though not necessary, to process this data. Refer to Exhibit 3–6 for a listing of computer software for customer surveys.

- Calculate the customer satisfaction score as follows: Start with the first question (Parking, for example). Take the expectations met response (let's say 3) and the importance response (let's say 4) and find these numbers (in bold type) on the following customer satisfaction scoring matrix.

		Low 1	2	3	High 4
				Importance	
Expectations Met	1 Not at all	-1.5	-3.0	-4.5	-6.0
	2	-.5	-1.0	-1.5	-2.0
	3	.5	1.0	1.5	**2.0**
	4 Exceeded	1.5	3.0	4.5	6.0

Note that these numbers intersect at 2.0. This is the customer satisfaction score for parking. Do this for each question on every survey. Find the corresponding CS score for each expectations met and importance score in the customer satisfaction scoring matrix.

The last step is to find the average CS score for each question among all surveys. List these average CS scores in descending order with the best score at the top. Which area shows the lowest CS score? Which area shows the second lowest? Which area shows the third lowest?

• Organize customer comments as follows: Concentrate on the negative comments written on the customer surveys. Group similar comments together and label each category.

For example, any remark about the behavior or personality of an employee can be classified under employee attitudes. This could be further separated by department (e.g., salespersons' attitudes) if there are many comments about that area. The idea is to come up with categories (stay under 10) that describe the majority of customers' concerns.

List your comment categories and how many customers made remarks pertaining to these areas. Which category had the largest number of critical comments? The second largest number? Do these comments relate to the three lowest CS scores identified above? If yes, which ones?

• Now, you're prepared to *select the general focus* of the project. Give preference to the area that has the biggest potential for improving customer satisfaction. This is an area that has a low expectations met (EM) score and a high importance (I) score.

To find this area, calculate the average EM and I scores for each of the three lowest CS scores. List these low-scoring areas and their corresponding EM and I scores. Which shows the lowest EM score and the highest I score? Label this *critical area 1*. Which area shows the second lowest EM score and the second highest I score? Label this *critical area 2*. Which shows the third lowest EM score and the third highest I score? Label this *critical area 3*.

• *Other considerations* in selecting the general focus include selecting an area that (1) you believe needs improvement, (2) you believe will gain sufficient attention and resources, and (3) you or an associate have sufficient knowledge of so that you will be able to consider the alternatives and implications of any proposed change.

Do *not* select an area that is currently being worked on (i.e., the problem is already being addressed).

Select the area with the next best score.

d. General focus. Identify your general focus on the basis of the low-scoring areas identified above, critical comments, the low-scoring area with the highest potential for improvement, and other considerations as discussed above.

Judgment Call

The idea is to select one area of concentration. You will be able to address the other areas after completing all of the steps for one area. Repeating these steps is the basis for continuous improvement.

Example: The results of a Toys "R" Us customer survey showed "easy to find toys" and "available salespeople" with the lowest CS scores. Toys "R" Us had recently increased the number of salespersons and initiated a program requiring these employees to wear bright-red smocks. It was decided, therefore, that the general focus should be to make it easier for customers to find toys.

What is your general focus?

Checklist
Before proceeding you should have:
____ Written a customer cycle.
____ Conducted a general customer survey.
____ Calculated customer satisfaction scores.
____ Identified your general focus.

Step 1—Getting Started

- Select your objective.
- Create a customer subcycle.
- List the steps needed to accomplish the objective.
- Gather background information.

Your time frame: _____ week. Your deadline: _____.

I. Selecting your objective. This involves the following actions:

a. Refer to the general focus (from Preliminary Step).

b. Rewrite your general customer cycle (from Preliminary Step).

c. Meet with a manager or a senior employee interested in this program to help determine the objective for this program. This discussion should focus on: (1) the customer cycle, (2) the general focus, and (3) comments made by customers in the preliminary survey.

Refine the general focus by agreeing on a specific area that represents the biggest potential for improving overall customer satisfaction. This area is the objective for the program. For example, if your general focus is food and beverage, your objective might be room service.

Judgment Call

Identify the objective for your program by focusing on one overriding problem that you will address. An example objective is "Create customer friendly return policies and procedures" (McCaulaou's Department Store customer satisfaction study, 1993).

What is your objective?

d. Create a customer subcycle. The subcycle allows you to take a closer look at the parts of the customer experience that you are interested in improving. This can include the customer (consumption) side, or the business (production) side.

- *The customer side*—Which steps in your general customer cycle (from *b*, above) are most closely related to your objective? Expand one or several of these steps into their component parts. For example, if step 4, room service, in the customer cycle for a hotel was most closely related to your objective, then the corresponding customer subcycle might look like this:

The Customer Subcycle (customer perspective)

1. Guest calls room service.
2. Places order.
3. Answers door; talks with server; signs bill.
4. Consumes food and beverage.
5. Sets tray outside door for pickup.
6. Reviews room service charges at checkout.

This is simply a more detailed look at the customer experience.

- *The business side*—Which production steps correspond to this customer subcycle? Internal production steps directly support the customer side. For example, the production steps for step 4, room service, might look like this:

The Production Subcycle (business's perspective)

1–2. Switchboard staff trained for order taking.
  3. Staff trained on the job in service techniques; uniforms required.
  4. Kitchen staff instructed on consistent preparation of all menu items.
  5. Housekeeping coordinated with room service staff for timely pickup of trays.
  6. Charges posted to guest hotel bill.

These are the activities, procedures, or tasks necessary to create the customer experience. List the production steps coinciding with your customer subcycle.

The customer and production subcycles, together, represent your *customer service cycle*.

II. Designing your program. Discuss with the manager what the desired outcomes are for the program. These are the benefits that will result from the program. For example, if the objective of a program is to upgrade a hotel's telephone system, then the desired outcomes might be that:

- Complaints would be reduced by 90 percent.
- Guest expectations would be exceeded and overall customer satisfaction would increase.
- Customers would take special notice of the added features and efficiency of the new system. It could be a useful advertising and promotional tool.

What are the desired outcomes for your program?

III. Researching your objective. Now that you have defined your objective and have support within your organization, the next step is to find current literature dealing with the subject of your program.

For example, if your program objective deals with employee motivation, then find recent articles and other material relating to these areas. If your program deals with increasing business from a current customer segment, then find current material dealing with customer segmentation and target marketing. Refer to Exhibit 7–4 for a list of resources. What did you find out from these resources?

Summarize how this information relates to your program. How will you use this information?

List your major customers by segment. How will each of these groups benefit from this program? These customer benefits may be useful to defend your efforts as you progress through this program.

Checklist
Before proceeding you should have:

_____ Identified your objective.

_____ Created a customer and production subcycle.

_____ Collected information on objective (articles, other material).

_____ Listed customer segment benefits from this program.

Step 2—Customer Satisfaction Components

- Identify expectation creators.
- Define current quality standards.
- Surface differences in perception.

Your time frame: _____ weeks. Your deadline: _____.

I. Customer expectations. The perception of superior performance can be eroded when preceded by exaggerated promises or misleading information. Organizations can affect customer expectations by understanding how they're created. By knowing what it is about products and services, advertising, pricing policies, reputation, and service quality (Exhibit 2–1) that are most significant and remembered by customers, companies can focus on these elements to create or modify expectations.

a. Rewrite the customer side of your cycle (refer to Step 1).

  b. How does the reputation of your entire organization affect the
      customer expectations associated with the products and services
      represented in this cycle?

  c. Briefly describe how the products and services related to the above
      cycle are currently represented in:

   • Advertising and promotions.

   • Store front and signage (packaging).

   • Image, decor, ambience, or status.

   • First impressions of employees and other customers.

   • Other in-store merchandising.

This information will be used in Step 3 to locate the origins of specific
customer expectations.

II. Quality. The purpose here is to identify existing quality
standards, and measure current performance to compare with existing
quality standards.

Quality standards promote consistency and excellence by providing
direction and motivation for employees. Superior performance is more
likely achieved when quality standards are clearly communicated, connected to employees' evaluation system, and represent customers' expectations (Step 5).

Do quality standards exist for any steps of your current customer service cycle? Remember, this represents the steps in the customer and producer subcycles. If any exist, identify them now so you can determine if
current performance meets these prescribed standards. You will use this
information in Step 5 to develop quality standards and employee programs
that will support your redesigned customer cycle.

*Judgment
Call*

  a. Rewrite your customer service cycle with any existing
      quality standards for each step. Express these in terms of
      cost, quality (specifications), and time, as done in the
      following examples.

   • *Example 1*—Pizza delivery.

   Quality: Delivered with the correct ingredients, hot, and
            undamaged.

Time: Within 15 minutes of phone call.

Cost: Delivery costs under 20 percent of total check.

- *Example 2*—Billing process.

Quality: Average percent of past-due receivables.

Time: Average time between bills sent out and collections received.

Cost: Labor, materials, and overhead total less than 5 percent of collections.

In creating standards, quality is often the most difficult to measure. Some measures of quality include number of complaints, error rate, efficiency, or warrantee and guarantee costs (refer to examples above and to Chapter 4 for additional help). These measures are necessary for making accurate comparisons with competitors in Step 4 and for creating new quality standards in Step 5.

If you have no quality standards, skip this section.

Go to Section III of this step.

Judgment Call

List existing quality standards for each step of your customer service cycle (this includes both subcycles). Complete this list for each step in your customer service cycle.

b. After identifying your current quality standards, assess their effectiveness by conducting a basic performance evaluation.

- Measure current performance. Using simple observation techniques and a cursory review of available information, identify the current quality, time, and cost for each of the steps listed above. Complete this list for each step in your customer service cycle.

- Compare the results with existing quality standards. The difference between your current quality standards and measures of current performance are your performance gaps. Based on these performance gaps, which steps appear to have the largest problem?

III. Priority marketing. The purpose of this part of Step 2 is to see how in touch employees and management are with customer satisfaction. Are they aware of how they best or least satisfy their customers? You'll use this information in Step 5 to assess how management and employee misperceptions will affect the implementation and success of the redesigned process.

  a. Customers are more satisfied with certain aspects of your products and services than with others. For example, in their experience with a particular brand of bread, customers may be most satisfied with freshness, nutrition, and price (in that order). On the other hand, they may be dissatisfied with the length of the bread's shelf life, the packaging, and loaf size. Refer back to your survey in the Preliminary Step. Which area showed the highest CS score? The second highest CS score? The lowest? The second lowest?

  b. How aware are employees of these attitudes? Select three to five employees. Include both front line workers and back-office workers. Combine the four aspects identified above in a single list, in a different order, and make a copy for each employee. Ask them to rank order the items according to how well they think customers are currently being satisfied, from 1, satisfied, to 4, dissatisfied. Do not reveal the customer rankings until they have completed the exercise.

   Combine the employees' answers by adding their rankings. If, for example, one employee ranked price first, another ranked it second, and another fourth, you would add up their rankings: $1 + 2 + 4 = 7$. After doing this for each item, rank order the results. Put the highest number of points on the bottom line.

  c. How does management's perception compare to that of customers and employees? Using the same customer generated list (*a*), ask several managers (the higher their status, the better) to rank order the items according to how well they think customers are currently being satisfied, from 1, satisfied to 4, dissatisfied. Combine the managers' answers by adding up their rankings. Once again, do not reveal the customer or employee rankings until they have completed the exercise. Rank order the results.

  d. Identify differences in perception. Compare the results of *a*, *b*, and *c* using a format similar to the example below. Returning to our bread example, customers may be most satisfied with freshness and nutrition, and least satisfied with the price and the package. Employees, however, may think that customers are satisfied with these in a slightly different order: (1) price, (2) freshness, (3) nutrition, and (4) package. Management may have their own opinion about customers' satisfaction: (1) price, (2) nutrition, (3) package, and (4) freshness. This can be seen in the following table:

Perceptions of Satisfaction

Aspects	Customer Ranking	Employee Ranking		Management Ranking		Perception Gap
Fresh	1	2		4		
		off by 1	+	off by 3	=	4
Nutrition	2	3		2		
		off by 1	+	off by 0	=	1
Price	3	1		1		
		off by 2	+	off by 2	=	4
Package	4	4		3		
		off by 0	+	off by 1	=	1

For each customer ranking we calculated a perception gap: the difference between actual customer satisfaction and how employees and management *think* customers are being satisfied. For example, the gap for fresh was figured as follows:

- How far off is the employee ranking from the customer ranking? By 1.
- How far off is the management ranking from the customer ranking? By 3.
- Adding these together: 1 + 3, equals the perception gap: 4.

The highest gap is where the biggest difference in perception, regarding customer satisfaction, exists within your company. The perception gap total would be as follows: freshness (4), nutrition (1), price (4), package (1).

Employees or management may *think* they're providing customer satisfaction, but inaccurate perceptions may be affecting their efforts. Persons often respond on the basis of their own perceptions. Personal biases of employees and managers often affect their own customer satisfaction efforts. Now, calculate the perception gaps using your results.

e. The highest perception gap is where the biggest difference in
   perception, regarding customer satisfaction, exists within your
   company. Rank order the perception gaps.
   Step 5 will utilize this information to anticipate where special
   attention may be needed in the design and implementation of
   changes in your customer service cycle.

Checklist
Before proceeding you should have:

____ Identified potential expectation creators.

____ Defined current quality standards, if any.

____ Measured current performance levels and performance
gaps.

____ Uncovered perception gaps among customers, employ-
ees, and managers regarding customer satisfaction.

Step 3—Customer and Employee Input

* A customer feedback exercise.
* An employee feedback exercise

Your time frame: _____ weeks. Your deadline: _____.

I. The customer feedback exercise. The purpose of collecting
feedback is to engage customers in helping to achieve your objective for
this program (stated in Step 1).

Decide which method to use for obtaining feedback. Some of the most
common methods are listed in Exhibit 3–1 and the guidelines for selecting
the best methods appear in Exhibit 3–2.

For illustration purposes, we will use focus groups. In this example we
will conduct two focus groups: the first with customers, the second with
employees. This approach is an excellent complement to the customer survey conducted in the Preliminary Step.

The customer focus group. This should be composed
of 6 to 12 customers. These customers should ideally represent
major customer segments or your best customers who have had
Judgment experience with your objective. For example, reviewing the
Call surveys from the Preliminary Step may reveal customer seg-

ments or individuals likely to have encountered the problems you want to solve. Contact these or similar customers to participate. You may wish to hold separate focus groups for each customer segment that is likely to have a distinct product or service experience.

Contact customers by mail, phone, or in person, whichever is more appropriate, and request their participation in this two- to three-hour exercise. Inform them that a gift will be provided as an incentive for their participation. Cash is often the best incentive. As a general guide, offer $50 for individual consumers, $75 for managers, and $200 for specialists such as medical professionals (refer to Chapter 3 for additional guidelines about incentives). Ask them to dress comfortably.

Hold the meeting in a pleasant place and serve light refreshments to foster the informal ambiance. Obtain a chalk board or other device for writing large notes. Also, secure a tape recorder or stationary video camera to record the session.

Judgment
Call

Select a moderator, such as an in-house trainer or outside professional. Avoid selecting an employee to be the moderator who is too familiar with the area being studied (he or she may influence the group). Select someone good at conducting meetings. Provide the moderator with (1) the material on customer expectations and quality (the results of Parts I and II of Step 2); and (2) a copy of this section of Step 3.

The moderator will conduct the focus group using the following guidelines:

1. Explain your objective and the importance of the focus group to the participants.

2. Have everyone write down a major problem or difficulty they have experienced that relates to your objective. Have them label it *key problem.*

3. Ask several individuals to explain their key problem to the group.

4. Ask participants to write their answers to the following regarding their own key problem: (*a*) "What did you expect?" (*b*) "Where did you get this notion from?" To help them answer this second question, read the following or read your responses from Step 2, I, *c*. Did you get this notion from:

   • Advertising and promotions? Please explain.

   • Store front and signage (and/or packaging)?

   • Image, decor, ambience, or status?

- Impressions of employees and other customers?
- Other in-store merchandising?
- Did anything else affect your expectations—for example, consistent quality and price, or reputation for new products and services?

5. Ask participants if they have experienced or know of better examples elsewhere. If so, ask them to write these down and mention them to the group.

6. Explain that the next step is very important. Ask participants to write down the ideal solution that would best resolve their problem. Tell them to imagine this solution without regard to cost or other restrictions. Have participants write these down and label it *ideal solution*.

   Optional questions:

   - Think of the steps you had to go through in terms of their importance to you.
   - Can this procedure be streamlined? Write down the steps that should be modified or eliminated.
   - Would any additional steps (services) be valuable? Write *additional step* next to these.

7. Ask several other individuals what their problem and ideal solutions were. Collect all papers from everyone.

8. Are there other areas, besides those focused on above that the group thinks need to be improved?

9. What do they like most about the company's products and services?

10. The moderator should review the customers' written materials to make sure he or she understands them. Ask customers for clarifications or further explanation if necessary.

Thank the customers for their input. Make sure they receive their incentive before leaving. Send a thank you letter or card to each participant.

Immediately following the focus group session, the moderator should complete a summary table similar to the one below. This information will be critical for the employee focus group.

Customer Focus Group—Summary Table

Dimension	Example
Key problem	Checkout takes too long
Segment	Business
Experience elesewhere	No check-out
Ideal solution	Send bill
CS cycle (eliminate/add/modify)	Eliminate checkout step

What were the most frequently mentioned key problems discussed in this session? How are expectations contributing to these problems? Refer to question 4*b*, "Where did you get this notion from?" List the specific expectation creators responsible (packaging, advertising, and so forth). You will need this information for the following employee focus group.

The employee focus group. The second focus group is composed of employees (internal customers).

Judgment Call

a. *Preparation.* First, list the three most frequently mentioned key problems discussed in the customer focus group. Which internal processes or procedures relate to these problems? Review the following example and then identify internal processes or procedures that the three key problems correspond to.

Key Problems	Internal Processes and Procedures
Checkout too long	Access guest file; create a bill; request guest approval of bill; resolve discrepancies; process payment; produce receipt; clear file; farewell script to guest.

Provide this list to the moderator before the beginning of the session. *Do not show this list to employees.*

Judgment Call

The group should be composed of 6 to 12 employees. Select Employees who are involved with the processes and procedures identified above. You should have at least two employees per process or procedure.

The purpose of this session is for employees to map out the internal steps that occur in these selected areas of operation. To encourage employee input and to avoid discomfort, the focus must remain on policies and procedures and not on individuals.

 Try to recruit the same moderator who conducted the customer focus group. Avoid selecting as a moderator an employee who is very familiar with the areas under consideration or who

Judgment might inhibit or influence employee input.
   Call

b. GUIDELINES

1. State your objective to this group; mention that it is based on the results of customer feedback.

2. Explain that the following processes or procedures relating to customers' key problems will be focused on in this session. Mention these processes, but do not (yet) identify the key problems to employees.

3. Ask employees to write at the top of a page which one of these they are most familiar with.

4. Now ask them to list all of the steps that are involved in the process or procedure they selected.

5. After completing their individual efforts, ask participants to join with others who were working on the same process or procedure. Together, ask them to create *one* comprehensive list of the steps involved in their process or procedure.

6. Now, reveal to participants the problem associated with their process or procedure. Ask them to think of what changes to the process or procedure would address this problem. Have them discuss the alternatives with their partners and then write down these options.

7. As a group, discuss the three problems and their solutions. The goal is to identify the best solution for each problem.

8. Have each group write down and label their best solution. Turn in one page per group to the moderator.

9. The moderator should review these written materials to make sure they understand them and ask employees for clarifications or further explanation if necessary.

10. Thank the employees for their input.

11. Send a thank you letter or card to each participant.

12. Immediately following this focus group session, the moderator should complete a summary table that includes the process or procedure, proposed changes, and best solution for each key problem.

c. ANALYSIS. Consider the results from both of the focus groups together. Briefly, what are the problems and solutions that surface as a result of these sessions? What else can you observe from the combined results of these two sessions?

The results from Step 3 (based on both of the focus group summary tables) will be used in Step 5 to:

- Identify sources of problems associated with your objective.
- Develop ideal solutions to these problems and ways to implement them.
- Integrate the results from this customer and employee input into specific plans for improvement.

Although we will directly address the most critical results of these focus groups in Step 5, an immediate response (supporting your efforts), could come in the form of a solution team. This group, made up of the moderators, managers, focus group employees, and other employees not involved in these sessions, can address some of the other issues brought up in these focus groups.

For additional information about conducting customer satisfaction focus groups, contact: Walker, CSM Inc. (800) 334-3939.

Checklist
Before proceeding you should have:

_____ Used customer feedback to determine key problems (related to your objective) experienced by customers.

_____ Listed customers' ideal solutions to these problems.

_____ Used employee feedback to solicit best solutions.

_____ Summarized the problems and solutions identified from this new customer and employee feedback.

Step 4—Competitive Advantage and Benchmarking

- Identify competitive advantage by focusing on your current strengths and weaknesses compared to other companies.
- Benchmark other companies to determine how you can achieve competitive superiority.

    Your time frame: _____ weeks. Your deadline: _____.

I. Competitive advantage

Judgment Call

a. Identify your company's two main competitors. From 0 to 10, rate each of the following aspects for your company and your two main competitors (0 = no advantage, 10 = big advantage): product advantage; service advantage; location advantage; price/value advantage; effectiveness of advertising/promotion, and growth potential.

b. Based on the above, that is, how well or poorly you stack up, list your most significant competitive advantages. For example, if you are Company X with two major competitors, part of your scoring sheet might look like this:

	Company X	Competitor 1, Company Y	Competitor 2, Company Z
Price/value advantage	9	3	4
Service advantage	8	6	7

In this example, your biggest advantages are for price and service.

Now complete this exercise by estimating your company's situation. Use your company's real figures whenver possible.

c. What is your biggest advantage? Your second biggest advantage? Again, referring to the above, what are your competitive disadvantages? Where are your numbers the lowest compared to your two competitors?

What is your biggest disadvantage? Your second biggest disadvantage?

Will this customer satisfaction program address these weaknesses? How? If not, what is being done, or could be done, to address these weaknesses?

II. The benchmarking procedure. Benchmarking focuses on keeping or achieving competitive advantage. It means, quite literally, "learning from your competitors" (see Exhibit 4–1).

Judgment Call

a. Your objective is really a process. A process links related tasks to yield a product or service to customers. Some examples of customer processes include product development, sales, order fulfillment, and billing. If your objective needs to be restated to represent a process, how would it be written?

In this Step we will refer to your objective as a process.

b. Refer back to Step 2, II, for the quality standards you have already identified for each step of your cycle. (If your organization has no standards for the process that you wish to benchmark, you will measure your current performance in *e* below.) *No comparison will be possible until you have measured your own process.*

c. When seeking a benchmarking partner, it may be necessary to offer them a look at one of your successful processes.
   1. Where does your organization excel? For example, what were the two competitive advantages you identified in the previous section, I*a*? What processes do these relate to?
   2. List three processes you believe your organization excels at; indicate what evidence there is to demonstrate this superiority.
   3. Cross out the process your company would not be willing to share with a benchmarking partner.
   4. Be prepared to demonstrate the cost, quality, and time for each of these processes.

d. Find several companies that excel at the process you are interested in benchmarking (identified in item 1, above). This search for leading examples can include the following:
   • Asking managers in your company for recommendations.

Judgment Call
   • Seeking the advice from the person in charge of this process at a competing company.

   • Using various benchmarking resources (Exhibit 4–3).

   • Reviewing trade and industry publications and calling their editorial staffs.

   • Contacting industry associations.

   • Calling the market leader in another industry.

Assemble a list of the potential companies you wish to benchmark. Describe their approach to the process. Why are they worth benchmarking?

e. From these examples, select a benchmarking partner that fits your situation; it's OK to adapt or scale this partner to your situation, if necessary. See Chapter 4 for techniques to persuade a potential company to become a benchmarking partner. It is also possible to select an organization to benchmark without their permission, as discussed in Chapter 4.

If your organization has no standards for the process that you wish to benchmark, you must measure your current performance before proceeding. First, find out what *units* your potential benchmarking partner uses to define its own performance for the process you're interested in. Then, using these same units, measure your own process. Actively observe or solicit information about the quality, time, and cost dimensions for each step (as appropriate) of your customer service cycle. Remember, this includes all of the steps in your customer and production subcycles.

Complete this list for each step in your customer service cycle.

f. Collect information on your benchmarking partner's process through site visits or consultants. Exhibit 8–1 presents a site visit worksheet.

g. Close the competitive gap between this leader and you by focusing on how they currently outperform your organization's process. This negative competitive gap represents the real improvement opportunity. Identify how your organization can close the gap by improving its knowledge, practices and processes.

h. Program future performance levels by benchmarking the expected future leader. Select a course of action (using and revising their processes where appropriate) that will allow you to reach and overtake the programmed leading level. Where will they be in one year in terms of cost, quality, and time? In three years? Five years?

To reach your objective for this program, which area(s) will need the most attention: quality, cost, time, or the customer service cycle? Again, focusing on your objective for this program, what action can you take to improve performance in these areas?

i. After identifying how your program can benefit from this benchmarking exercise, the challenge is to integrate these contributions into your operation. Using customer, employee, and competitor information, Step 5 will help you redesign the customer service cycle according to your program's objective. Step 5 will also match human resource approaches that will support your redesigned customer service cycle as well as other companywide employee issues. Step 6 capitalizes on these improvements by developing a customer loyalty program and a satisfaction guarantee tailored to needs of your product and service mix. And finally, Step 7 will consider technological applications and other expansion opportunities for your World-class Customer Satisfaction Program.

EXHIBIT 8–1
Site Visit Worksheet

1. Name of company you are benchmarking: _____

2. Name of contact person: _____

3. Process you are benchmarking: _____

4. Measures of your own process:　　　　　Quality　_____

　　　　　　　　　　　　　　　　　　　　Time　_____

　　　　　　　　　　　　　　　　　　　　Cost　_____

(use additional pages if necessary)

5. Rewrite your customer service cycle (from Step 1):

Customer steps (consumption)	Service steps (production)
1. _____	1. _____
2. _____	2. _____
3. _____	3. _____
4. _____	4. _____
5. _____	5. _____
6. _____	6. _____
7. _____	7. _____
8. _____	8. _____

6. Collect background information on the company you are benchmarking. For example, what's so great about its process that you're interested in benchmarking? Does that company suffer in other areas as a result of being superior in this one process? Background information: _____
_____

7. Visit the company in a three-person team. While one asks questions, one notes the answers and the third thinks of the next question. The questions should center on:

Best practices (current and planned):
_____
_____
_____

(continued)

EXIIIBIT 8–1
Site Visit Worksheet

(continued)

Measures: Costs of inputs _____

                   Quality of outputs _____

                   Cycle time of outputs _____

Identify the customer service cycle steps of

    Their process: _____

Customer steps (consumption)	Service steps (production)
1. _____	1. _____
2. _____	2. _____
3. _____	3. _____
4. _____	4. _____
5. _____	5. _____
6. _____	6. _____
7. _____	7. _____
8. _____	8. _____

Additional (or clarifying) information needed:

_____

_____

8. Plans to obtain missing information:

_____

_____

_____

9. Immediately following your visit, conduct a debriefing meeting with your team.
   What are the biggest differences between your process and their process (quality,
   time, cost, or steps in the customer service cycle)?

_____

_____

_____

_____

(continued)

EXHIBIT 8–1   *(concluded)*
Site Visit Worksheet

How can your company benefit from these differences?

_____

_____

_____

Checklist
Before proceeding you should have:
_____ Identified the most significant advantage and disadvantage compared to your main competitors.
_____ Recognized the process relating to your objective.
_____ Visited a company that excels at this process.
_____ Determined how this company's process is superior and what can be applied to your organization.
_____ Selected measurable goals for managing improvement into the future.

Step 5—Designing World-Class Customer Satisfaction

- Improve your customer process with customer, employee, and competitor input.
- Include the latest developments in human resource management as a vital component of this new process.

    Your time frame: _____ weeks. Your deadline: _____.

    We all understand the basic notion of customer satisfaction: making customers feel good about their purchases. But understanding the concept is very different than knowing what should be done, deciding how to do it, or actually doing it. We'll deal with this in two ways:

- Redesign—By focusing on a single customer process you will be able to integrate the results from customer, employee, and competitor input into specific plans for improvement.

- Best employee practices—By tailoring employee programs to support reengineered processes you will use the latest developments in human resource management to get employees more involved and also address their professional and personal development.

Redesign.   The objective will be to modify the elements that are contributing to dissatisfaction (e.g., poor customer treatment and confusing pricing), add ingredients that will enhance satisfaction (superior customer handling and customer-friendly pricing), and combine them into a new presentation of customer-valued products and services including a streamlined customer experience. These steps—reshaping products, personnel, procedures, technology, management priorities, or cost, all in the name of customer satisfaction—is what redesign is all about. This is also called *reengineering*.

The redesign steps are as follows:

- Focus on the problem.
- Identify causes.
- Consider alternative courses of action.
- Redesign for customer satisfaction.

I. Focus on the problem.   What is the biggest problem in achieving your objective according to (*a*) customers (Preliminary Step and Step 1), (*b*) employees (from Step 3), and (*c*) competitor comparisons (from Step 4)?

II. Identify causes.   What are the causes of the poor scores? Be careful not to jump to conclusions. If you are not completely knowledgeable about a part of the process you are evaluating, seek out assistance from others who are.

a. Based on the customer focus group summary table in Step 3, what could be causing the problems associated with your objective?

b. Based on this same table, how could expectations be contributing to the problems associated with your objective?

c. Based on the employee focus group summary table in Step 3, what else could be causing the problems associated with your objective?

Judgment Call

d. Examine the possible causes of this problem. Based on the input that you have accumulated, select the key problem related to your objective. Using a fishbone chart, identify and explain the root causes affecting this issue. Refer to Exhibit 5–2 for a fishbone example.

III. Consider alternative courses of action.

a. Which branches of the diagram are really causing the problem? Rank order them on a scale of 1, responsible, to 6, not responsible. Which barrier is most responsible for the overall problem?

b. Which customer generated ideal solutions from Step 3 would help to remove this barrier? What other customer input obtained in Step 3 supports your objective?

c. Which superior competitor practices from Step 4 relate to this barrier?

d. Using the suggested actions to remove internal barriers (refer to *a*, above), customers' ideal solutions (*b*, above), superior competitor practices (*c*, above) or other remedies, what can be done to make the whole process more customer friendly? List three alternatives, their corresponding pros and cons, and their overall impact.

Which has the best net payoff? How can this alternative be pursued? Could more than one alternative be realistically pursued?

IV. Redesign for customer satisfaction.
The customer service cycle completed in Step 1 includes one step or several steps negatively affecting your customers' satisfaction. This redesign procedure is aimed at correcting this. Let's review how it works with an example:

Room Service Customer Service Cycle

Customer perspective
1. Guest calls room service.
2. Places order.
3. Answers door; talks with server; signs bill.
4. Consumes food and beverage.
5. Sets tray outside door for pickup.
6. Reviews room service charges at checkout.

(continued)

Room Service Customer Service Cycle   *(concluded)*

Hotel perspective

1. Staff trained for efficient and courteous order taking.
2. Staff trained in service techniques; uniforms and equipment well maintained.
3. Kitchen staff instructed on consistent preparation of all menu items.
4. Housekeeping coordinated with room service staff for timely pickup of trays.
5. Charges posted to guest's hotel bill.

Judgment Call

Each step in the customer service cycle should contribute to customer satisfaction. If it doesn't, or contributes too little for its trouble, it should be eliminated or streamlined to reduce customer involvement. The choices for evaluating your cycle are therefore: modify steps, eliminate steps, combine steps, add steps, or do nothing.

a. Retrieve the customer service cycle completed in Step 1. Based on the customer input obtained in the Preliminary Step (CS scores), Step 3 (what steps are least important to customers?), and from your own experience, rank order how each step contributes to customer satisfaction.

Now, starting with the step that contributes the least to customer satisfaction (rank 1), complete the following:

1. In what ways do customers benefit from (or need) this step? Example: if "Step 5: Sets tray outside door for pickup," is ranked last, the customer benefits by staff getting rid of tray quickly. There would be no additional customer benefits. Label this Customer Benefit A.

   In what other ways do customers benefit from this step? Label these Customer Benefit B, Customer Benefit C, and so on.

2. In what ways does your organization benefit from, or need, this step? Example: The organization benefits by not having to worry about picking up the tray as soon as the guest is done. There are no additional customer benefits. Label this Organization Benefit A.

   In what other ways does your organization benefit from this step? Label these Organization Benefit B, Organization Benefit C, and so on.

   Now add the customer and organization benefits for the second and third lowest ranked steps and compare all three (you've already completed this for the lowest ranked step).

Reevaluate each step in terms of how it directly affects customer satisfaction. How can these steps be modified or eliminated to make this process more customer friendly?

Try combining those steps having only marginal value to customer satisfaction. Can any steps be combined or eliminated? How?

You may add steps if they will add to customer satisfaction. What additional steps may be taken to improve the customer experience?

Based on the above analysis construct a *new customer service cycle*. Remember to include both customer steps and corresponding service steps.

Judgment Call

To ensure that this cycle will be delivered effectively, you must develop quality standards. Each step of your redesigned customer service cycle needs to be explained with well-defined quality standards. On the basis of the following information, create quality standards for each step in your new customer service cycle. Do this by:

- Rewriting the quality standards already identified (Step 2, Part II).
- Listing customers' expectations and their ideal solutions (Step 3).
- Listing the best practices of competitors (Step 4) as they relate to your redesigned customer service cycle.

Now, using the information above, identify the quality standards for each step in your redesigned cycle that address your objective and are appropriate for your organization.

Judgment Call

To help define these quality standards, consider using the RATER dimensions of service quality (refer to Chapter 2). Make sure all of these dimensions are reflected in your quality standards: Reliability, Assurance, Tangibles, Empathy, Responsiveness. (Chapter 2 provides additional guidelines for developing new quality standards.)

Best employee practices. The ultimate success of your redesigned customer service cycle depends on the employees who will execute it. Before handing over this burden, however, incorporate certain employee programs within this redesign to help ensure that it will be carried out effectively. Aligning human resource practices with customer satisfaction initiatives may require revolutionary changes in the way organizations train, empower, evaluate, and reward individuals and teams. Matching the latest developments in human resource management to each step in the redesigned process is the purpose of rest of Step 5.

In the following example, Company X redesigned its customer service cycle and achieved its goal of increasing employee productivity by using innovative compensation and motivation techniques. As a result, individual workers participated in a greater range of work activities (recruitment and training) and improved overall output.

Company X's Employee Solutions to Match Redesigned Processes

New Step	How it affects employees	Best Practice
Kitchen staff delivers room service orders	Additional knowledge and skills required	Involve employees in recruitment; "cross-training"; "broadbanding"

The procedure you will follow to match human resource approaches to your redesigned customer service cycle requires four activities:

Judgment Call

a. Refer to the quality standards that you assigned (in the first part of Step 5) to each step in the redesigned cycle. Consider what will be required to deliver World-class customer satisfaction. Will employees be able to deliver these levels of quality? Think of the employees your redesigned customer service cycle will affect. What new or modified responsibilities will be given to these employees? Will there be the new expectations of their performance? For each new step of the redesigned process, identify how the change will affect employees (refer to the example of Company X above).

Judgment Call

b. From the employee best solutions listed in Exhibit 8–2, select one that will help employees adapt to these changes.

c. Find and complete the corresponding exercise in the remainder of this step for each approach selected.

d. If it still seems appropriate, collect more information about this technique. Chapter 5 briefly describes these approaches; Exhibit 5–8 provides a list of resources. Also use your own human resource department for support.

EXHIBIT 8–2
Employee Best Solutions

I. High Turnover ——> Increase Employee Loyalty

New recruitment efforts	Employees take greater role in screening and hiring process.
Employee orientation	Enhance future performance and help reduce turnover.
Career pathing	Plans for employees to receive training and development for advancement purposes.
Work-life	Known as employee assistance programs (EAPs): family life, dependent care and child care.
Long-term incentive and reward	Long-term evaluation of employee productivity focuses more on career development.

II. Low productivity ——> Improve Productivity and Quality

Employee involvement	EI programs encourage employee participation in planning how firm operates.
Team building	Efforts to foster teamwork and improve communication within organizations.
Empowerment	Power and authority is delegated to subordinates.
Pay for performance	Compensation based on the value added by employees to products and services.

III. Insufficient knowledge ——> Professional and Personal Development

Training and education	Demand for skilled workers requires new investments, innovative techniques, and effective controls.
Cross-training	Employees trained to perform functions of personnel in another area of organization.
Broadbanding	Multiple salary grades reduced for greater worker flexibility.

As you select from the latest employee programs (Chapter 5) for their ability to support your redesigned cycle, consider how likely they are to be expanded and adapted in other areas of your organization. These are the programs and techniques you should focus on in this redesign step.

Solutions for increasing employee loyalty. Employee loyalty is at an all time low.[2] The principal reason workers leave a job is they lack an incentive to stay. Their needs are not being met: they are not recognized sufficiently and often have little opportunity for a career path.

Although all of the material in this step will support employee loyalty, certain programs devoted exclusively to this purpose are essential. Referring to the corresponding material in Chapter 5, explain how each of the following can be improved to support your objective.

- Quality recruitment.
- Meaningful orientation.
- Realistic career opportunities: career pathing.
- Work-life programs.
- Long-term incentive and reward systems.

Judgment Call

Solutions for improving productivity and quality. Low productivity and poor quality continue to challenge many organizations; but fortunately, many of the advancements in human resource management address these concerns. Some of these include team management, worker empowerment, and skill-based pay (see Exhibit 5–9).

- *Teamwork*—Teams are the building block of world-class organizations. Supervisory roles are limited by making groups manage themselves. They are given a clear purpose and are held accountable for measurable performance goals.

  Cross-functional teams are becoming more popular because of their unique problem solving abilities. How does your company currently use this approach?

  Based on the first and second biggest employee problem that you identified above, create a team approach that would benefit the customer. What would be the team's purpose? Which employees would be involved? What would be the team performance goals?

- *Alternative schedules*—How would a compressed workweek or a flextime approach to scheduling employees address the critical employee issues that you identified above? (Refer to Chapter 5, "Alternative Schedules").

- *Employee compensation*—Measure performance on the basis of the value created by implementing innovative incentive pay systems. By figuring out how much individuals actually contribute to products and services, you can pay employees according to their value-added contributions. Whether or not any incentive pay or reward systems currently exist in your organization, consider using the latest developments in these approaches.

Using the guidelines on incentive pay and rewards presented in Chapter 5, which components of these systems would address the critical employee issues? Give special emphasis to those systems that may hold potential for expanding into other parts of your organization.

Now, refer to the new quality standards you defined above. How can the components of these incentive pay and reward systems directly support the standards in your redesigned customer service cycle?

Which approaches provide the best support for your redesigned customer service cycle? Collect more information about how these compensation systems work. Resources are listed in Exhibit 5–7.

- Rewards—The employees who were responsible for contributing to the areas receiving the highest customer satisfaction scores or mentioned in the comments of the Preliminary Step survey should be recognized.

    What can you do to recognize or reward these and other outstanding employees?

    How can a recognition and reward system support the compensation programs identified above?

- Empowerment—What is the best example of employee empowerment in your organization? How could this approach be expanded to other personnel?

Employee involvement includes all of the approaches discussed above: teamwork, scheduling, compensation, reward systems and empowerment. The idea is to move decisions to the lowest level in the organization. How will your organization support these efforts? (See Exhibit 5–2.)

Top management—Who?

Middle management—Who?

A "champion" (program advocate)—Who?

Resources—Which? How much?

A clear objective—What is it?

Judgment Call

Solutions for improving professional and personal development. Although technology and employee incentives support training and development efforts, new demands for knowledge and budget cutting have made companies very discriminating in their approach to training and development.

- *Training and development*—How does your organization currently provide or encourage employee training and development? How do these programs tie directly to your organization's objectives? How could training and development be improved? (Refer to Chapter 5, "Training and Development")

  Describe any long-term or on-going development programs. How could these be improved?

  Are there any specific programs for minorities/women? How could these be improved?

- *Cross-training*—Cross-training (training employees to perform functions in another area of their organization) is effective in improving the relationships between internal customers and increasing employees' organizational awareness.

  Which areas or departments are highly dependent on each other? For example, finance personnel might depend on the results of the sales department or service might rely heavily on production. Suggest to the managers of these areas that they try a cross-training exercise (Chapter 5).

  How can the benefits of cross-functional teams support your program's objective?

  Another approach to cross-training is for employees to role-play the customer experience. To improve customer understanding, you or other workers should complete as much of the customer experience as possible. A primary objective is to learn how your own work affects the entire customer experience. Which departments do you have the most contact with?

  Select two of these departments, one known for its effectiveness in dealing with customers, the other, for its problems in satisfying customers. Approach these departments as a real customer (or enlist the help of a "stranger"), and up to a point, engage in transactions just like a regular customer. Write the customer cycle for each of these experiences. In terms of customer satisfaction, what were the good and not-so-good aspects of these experiences? How can these departments (yours and the other two) work together to provide better customer satisfaction?

What other new ideas in management (Exhibit 5–9) could support your objective? How can you investigate these new ideas further? Exhibit 5–7 provides a list of resources. Other approaches for you to explore include talking with others in your organization and contacting local trade/industry associations and other personnel/human resource management organizations. What are your plans for investigating these "new ideas"?

Refer back to Step 2, Part III. Where were the biggest perception gaps (the difference between actual customer satisfaction and what employees and management think satisfies customers)? Rank order the perception gaps. The biggest perception gap is where the largest difference in perception, regarding customer satisfaction, exists within your company. How could these perception gaps affect the implementation of the redesigned process and new or modified employee practices?

Checklist

Before proceeding you should have:

____ Determined the sources of customer and employee problems.

____ Identified alternatives to improving the current customer service cycle based on customer's ideal solutions, employees' best solutions, and competitors' superior practices.

____ Evaluated and then redesigned your customer service cycle and created new quality standards.

____ Selected employee practices that directly support the changes made in your new cycle.

Step 6—Retention Marketing

- Maximize repeat business with a customer loyalty program.
- Create a satisfaction guarantee.

Your time frame: _____ weeks. Your deadline: _____.

I. Customer loyalty. For businesses, creating and keeping repeat customers is essential:

- Loyal customers do wonders for improving cash flow. They make repeat purchases over a long period of time.
- It costs less to keep a customer than to gain a new one—up to five times less.

- Repeat customers are more willing to pay higher prices for products and services. They also spend more than first time customers.
- Current customers bring in new customers. Nothing works better than a personal recommendation.
- If they're not your customers, their patronage belongs to someone else.

Customer loyalty begins with a first purchase; when the customer concludes that there is no better choice, a strong and enduring relationship develops. When a company executes its processes properly, people move up this loyalty ladder from trial buyer, to client, to advocate (Exhibit 6–1). Barriers to moving up this loyalty ladder include:

- *Switching costs*—Price of changing patronage habits. This includes search costs, transaction costs, learning costs, loyal customer discounts, customer habit, emotional cost, and physical and mental effort.
- *Perceived risks*—Unknown component of new purchase. These include the financial, social, and psychological risks associated with the purchase of a new product or service.
- Lack of information—Information about current market alternatives. This includes lack of knowledge about your product, your competitor, and the general market.

a. How do the following barriers apply to purchases of your products and services? Refer to above definitions and Exhibit 6–1.
- Switching costs.
- Perceived risks.
- Lack of information.

    How can each of the barriers above be reduced?

b. What benefits do loyal customers receive as a result of their repeated purchases of your products and services (e.g., more flexible payment arrangements, free catalogs, announcements of new products, familiarity with employees)? How could each of these be increased?

    These benefits can form the basis of a frequent buyer program. What more could be offered to customers as an incentive for remaining loyal to your company's products and services (providing loyal customers with a bigger advantage or increased value)? For example, miles are the preferred currency of most frequent buyer programs. If you can't become associated with an existing mileage program, establish one of your own with a complete menu of awards. The prize list should be made up of valuable core products and services, not green stamps or trivial gifts.

Select a currency (miles, points, number of visits, dollars spent) that customers will accumulate to earn the awards listed above.

Judgment Call c. Explain how each of the following can be included in your frequent buyer program (Refer to I*a* above).

- How can your loyalty program help to reduce the three barriers to customer loyalty?

- How can the enhanced benefits that loyal customers receive as a result of their repeated purchases of your products and services be part of your loyalty program?

- How will you ensure that your program includes the six keys to a successful frequent-buyer program: effective, simple, convenient, fun, memorable, profitable?

Now go back to the Preliminary Step, Section IIIc. Which two areas had the lowest customer satisfaction scores? What were the two most frequently mentioned critical comments? What were the two most frequently mentioned reasons that some customers were not likely to return?

Based on the results from the Preliminary Step and the loyalty program you outlined above, what else is needed to preserve or encourage customer loyalty? How could this be included in your frequent buyer program?

Briefly describe how this simple customer loyalty program would work. What is the most significant benefit offered by this program to stimulate customer loyalty? Create a name for this customer loyalty program.

II. Service and satisfaction guarantees. Standing behind a restaurant meal, a car wash, or even a haircut with a clearly stated, hassle-free guarantee may be somewhat difficult to control, but it can offer a strong competitive advantage. More and more companies are depending on these programs not only for their marketing appeal, but for their impact on organizational effectiveness.

a. Using the sample format below, write a customer satisfaction guarantee that has real value. It can be the centerpiece of your entire operation or simply a promotional tool. Either way, make the guarantee unconditional, easy to invoke, and quick to pay.

100% Customer Satisfaction Guarantee

We pledge that you will be 100 percent satisfied with all (company name) products and services. If you're not completely satisfied with our (generic product name), you may (return, cancel, etc.) at any time for a full, 100 percent refund of every cent you paid. Not a prorated refund, but a complete refund of your entire price, even if _____ _____. No questions, no problems.

b. What is guaranteed? Is it clearly stated? Is this sufficient? Does it make sense?

Use the following guidelines to ensure that it will be an effective guarantee for you and your customer (refer to Exhibit 7–17 for more detail). A quality guarantee is:

- Legitimate—Make it unconditional and fair.
- Hassle-free—Make it easy to collect.
- Distinct—Call it something special like the "no-risk" guarantee.
- Forceful—If restrictions must apply, make them flexible and generous.
- Explicit—Spell out the guarantee. Avoid or minimize restrictions.
- Sincere—Don't use legal jargon, fine print, or asterisks.
- Obvious—Make it stand out. Print it large.

Finding out why customers are invoking a guarantee is also very important so that patterns may be easily identified and corrected. Have each person who collects on the guarantee, or an employee, fill out a brief card explaining the reason for invoking it.

Checklist
Before proceeding you should have:

_____ Identified the barriers currently surrounding your products and services that are reducing repeat business.

_____ Identified the benefits that are currently provided to your repeat customers.

_____ Designed a frequent buyer program that reduces barriers, offers enhanced benefits or awards, and has all the key dimensions of a successful program.

_____ Created a satisfaction guarantee that includes all of the key components.

Step 7—Trends

- Take advantage of technological developments.
- Capitalize on global trends in satisfaction that apply to your organization.

Your time frame: _____ weeks. Your deadline: _____.

What developments in technology and global markets can be integrated into your business? Refer to Chapter 7.

How can you take advantage of government assistance such *Judgment* as direct funding, tax reductions, and other resources? For tech-*Call* nology? For global expansion?

How can you expand your use of international resources pertaining to new markets, better information, or added products or services?

How will or could telephone technology improve your customers' satisfaction (refer to Chapter 7)? If you don't know, call the phone company's corporate or small-business representative. AT&T's public relations office is located at: Room 3B79, 99 Jefferson Road, Parsippany, NJ 07054, (201) 581-6947.

Checklist
In this step you should have:
_____ Identified general, technical, and global opportunities for your business.

_____ Investigated how government and other international resources can support these opportunities.

NOTES

1. Regina F. Maruca, "The Right Way to Go Global: An Interview with Whirlpool CEO David Whitman," Harvard Business Review, March–April 1994, p. 143.
2. Charles Solomon, "The Loyalty Factor," *Personnel Journal*, September 1992, p. 52.

Index

Thank you for choosing Irwin Professional Publishing for your business information needs. If you are part of a corporation, professional association, or government agency, consider our newest option: Irwin Professional Custom Publishing. This allows you to create customized books, manuals, and other materials from your organization's resources, select chapters of our books, or both.

Irwin Professional Publishing books are also excellent resources for training/ educational programs, premiums, and incentives. For information on volume discounts or Custom Publishing, call 1-800-634-3966.

Other books of interest to you from Irwin Professional Publishing . . .

CLOSE TO THE CUSTOMER
25 Management Tips from the Other Side of the Counter

James H. Donnelly, Jr.

A sometimes shocking, often humorous look at encounters between customers and organizations gives 25 ideas to use to keep customers coming back for more. (214 pages)
1-55623-569-0

TOTAL CUSTOMER SATISFACTION
Putting the World's Best Programs to Work

Jacques Horovitz and Michele Jurgens Panak

Explores the activities of global companies with excellent reputations for customer service. Practical examples and in-depth case studies from the best in the business will enable companies to give their customers the best in service quality. (275 pages)
0-7863-0108-2

AFTERMARKETING
How to Keep Customers for Life Through Relationship Marketing

Terry G. Vavra

Gives a clear mandate to help gain category leadership in the radically changing marketplace of the 90s. Includes ways to identify your customer and build a customer identification file. (292 pages)
1-55623-605-0

OPENING CLOSED DOORS
Keys to Reaching Hard-to-Reach People

C. Richard Weylman

This unique guide is filled with hundreds of practical tactics sales professionals (and business owners) can use to unleash the power of relationship-building in their marketing and prospecting efforts—and reap the benefits in increased acquisition of hard-to-reach customers and ultimately, more sales. (200 pages)
0-7863-0154-6